Gwynne Price

Clay Pigeon and Wing Shooting and the Gun and how to Use it ..

Gwynne Price

Clay Pigeon and Wing Shooting and the Gun and how to Use it ..

ISBN/EAN: 9783337162832

Printed in Europe, USA, Canada, Australia, Japan

Cover: Foto ©Lupo / pixelio.de

More available books at **www.hansebooks.com**

CLAY PIGEON AND WING SHOOTING,

AND

THE GUN AND HOW TO USE IT.

Advice to Young Sportsmen on Hunting, Shooting and Prevention of Accidents with Guns. New Rules for Clay Pigeon and Ground Trap Shooting. Objections to Plunge-Trap and Class Shooting. Instructions for Handicapping, Care of Pigeons, Etc.

BY

GWYNNE PRICE,

English Champion Wing Shot,

Contested with Capt. Bogardus for Championship of the World Gold Medal, in England, 1875, and at Indianapolis and St. Louis, 1876, and Defeated him at St. Louis in 1880.

PRICE, 25 CENTS.

Mailed Free, for Stamps, Gwynne Price, Rinkelville, St. Louis, Mo.

Wholesale: { AMERICAN NEWS CO., NEW YORK.
 ST. LOUIS NEWS CO., ST. LOUIS, MO.

Copyright, 1884, by Gwynne Price.

PREFACE.

"*THE GUN AND HOW TO USE IT, ETC.,*" was published about two years since, and was intended to afford instruction to *young* and *inexperienced gunners* only. Nearly twelve thousand copies have been distributed throughout the United States and Canada, and more than six hundred complimentary letters have been received, showing that it was appreciated.

The primary object of its publication, as may be gathered from the strong views expressed on the subject, was to bring about a *radical change* in Pigeon Trap-Shooting—to show the necessity of a better supply of live pigeons—and to advocate the total abolition of the *iniquitous* and *delusive* system of Class shooting.

I regret that my efforts have only partially succeeded in that direction, although I find such an under-current of public opinion on the subject that another season will bring about an altered state of things. It is only kept up now by the promoters of tournaments, who get them up for all the money there *can be made* out of it.

The birds supplied for the season of 1883, were much worse *than ever before*, as regards condition. In some instances tournaments were *postponed indefinitely* and the birds returned upon the dealers hands; in others, *dead* and *half-starved* birds were trapped, causing great dissatisfaction; the only wonder being that the Humane Society did not interfere where wounded birds were left ungathered.

Thanks, however, to the introduction of the Clay Pigeon, no difficulty need now be experienced in getting the finest possible practice in Wing Shooting *at a cheap rate*, more particularly so, whenever it becomes well understood.

In this little book I have endeavored to give some of my ideas on Clay Pigeon Shooting, and also some *New Rules*, which I think will be found of use and aid in making this sport popular.

GWYNNE PRICE.

CLAY PIGEON AND WING SHOOTING.

The first and principal object of Trap-Shooting should be the attainment of the nearest approach to perfection in the enjoyable and healthful recreation of Field shooting on the Wing.

No doubt, the practice obtained from the flight of the live pigeon, when flushed in a natural manner from a ground trap, is the best, but the difficulty of getting pigeons, *whether wild or tame*, in good condition, as well as the high price now paid for them, renders it a necessity that artificial means should be resorted to.

An inanimate object, propelled by mechanical means, is much cheaper, and naturally suggests itself as the *only* resource obtainable; but until very recently no invention has been made of sufficient utility to answer the purpose properly.

Every game bird is found upon the ground, and on being moved, makes an *upward* or *rising* flight, presenting, consequently, the most difficult of all shots, particularly so if slightly quartering. It is therefore a necessity, in order to become proficient as a wing shot, that a style of motion the *nearest approaching* to the ordinary flight of a bird, should always be used in practice.

Pigeons jerked from a plunge trap are generally shot at when falling, and the same may be said of glass balls thrown from *most* traps, such motion is therefore *diametrically opposed* to field shooting. Instead of such practice being beneficial in producing good field shots, it is exactly the reverse, for at game nearly every shot is a rising one.

Clay pigeon shooting, when the traps are set to throw the birds in every direction of quartering and straight-away slightly rising shots, is the only invention to the present time combining every element necessary to make fine game shots; and where the traps are set *according to instructions* and properly handled, will produce every style of shooting in imitation of the bird itself, of which it is the best possible substitute.

The clay pigeon and the trap which propels it at a terrific pace, are both the invention of Mr. George Ligowsky, of Cincinnati, who is a really representative sportsman and lover of a gun. He has worthily earned, not merely the barren honor of being the first to discover so good a substitute for live pigeon shooting, but he will undoubtedly reap a substantial reward in the near future.

Mr. Ligowsky has also, in experimenting in the manufacture of the clay saucer or pigeon, found a means by which pottery of any description can be moulded and shaped by machinery, instead of the hitherto only known method of hand labor, thereby ensuring great regularity.

In the early time of shooting at this funny substitute for a bird, complaints were pretty general that, although a saucer may have been struck by many shots, oftimes *it was not broken*, which may however, have arisen from other causes than irregularity of thickness of the clay; such as *want of penetration* from insufficient or *bad powder* or *wads*, or from shells being imperfectly loaded with improper proportions of ammunition. Latterly, however, there has been such regularity in the manufacture of the clays, that if not broken when struck, the cause may be looked for elsewhere.

Having been for nearly fifty years an ardent lover of field sports and trap shooting, and having expended probably more money in pigeons than any person now living, and never having until recently shot at an inanimate object from a trap, I must confess to having felt a great objection to both glass balls and clay pigeons when first introduced, because I saw that the motion of the glass ball was *injurious to wing practice*, except that of course, it drew attention to the necessity of making certain calculations, and it also helped to give steadiness to the nerves in public shooting.

My first experience with the clay pigeon, about two years since, was an unfortunate one, as dampness from a drizzling rain all day caused the the tips or handles to become loose in nearly every instance, and the traps being handled *by a novice*, acted so annoyingly that I gave it up in disgust, and did not see any more clays shot at until last summer.

From the few *proper shots* I saw made I was satisfied that the principle *was correct;* and having since had opportunity of seeing some shooting properly managed, I am satisfied now that it is *the thing of the future*, and that it will be very extensively in use this season.

Shooting from five traps, the plan I have very strenuously advocated, is certain to be generally adopted by representative sportsmen, and I notice the Ligowsky Co. offer special inducements in lowering the price of the traps in sets of five, or to complete the set. I hope, however, that the cost will be still further reduced, as I fail to see the necessity of throwing the birds at different elevations; as if thrown at an elevation of about 20 feet at 40 yards from the trap, so that only the edge is exposed to the charge, it is *certainly all required.*

A record of 90 in 100, at 15 yards rise, in the third notch, with an elevation of 75 degrees, which presents almost a full view of the bird, and in which case the bird travels *much slower*, so as to be almost stationary at 30 yards, is not equal to a score of 70 with a good spring in the fourth notch and an elevation of 20 degrees.

For early practice I recommend *short rises* at clays, as they travel much faster than a bird, and make very difficult shooting at first; a really good record can only be made with *great quickness* and *accuracy of aim.*

I was present lately at a public exhibition given by a celebrated shot, where the traps were so *manipulated* that it would be a farce to call it shooting, such as it was skill; being somewhat equivalent to aiming at a *miniature balloon* at 30 yards; the bird being thrown almost perpendicular, consequently meeting the wind, it was almost standing still.

In any published report of a contest, in order to ascertain the degree of merit, a full account should be given of the *number of traps, how far apart, what notch, elevation at 40 yards*, and *at what rise.* Where these particulars are omitted the report is practically valueless, and is passed over as worthless by those most interested.

A few poles 20 feet high at 40 yards from the traps will show at a glance if the elevation is correct.

The following records may be interesting, if only for encouragement, and to show that great scores can be made with practice.

Dr. Carver and Captain Bogardus gave twenty-five exhibition shoots under the auspices of the Clay Pigeon Company. Conditions: 100 birds each, 18 yards rise, English rules, use of both barrels, traps fourth notch, as follows:

	CARVER.	BOGARDUS.
Chicago,	72	63
St. Louis,	85	69
Cincinnati,	89	74
Kansas City,	91	69
St. Joseph,	92	63
Leavenworth,	85	63
Omaha,	94	90
Council Bluffs,	96	96
Des Moines,	100	97
Davenport,	95	89
Burlington,	99	99
Quincy,	100	92
Peoria,	98	92
Terre Haute,	99	95
Indianapolis,	98	97
Dayton, O.,	94	94
Columbus,	76	93
Pittsburg,	94	95
Philadelphia,	96	95
Jersey City,	98	94
New Haven,	96	82
Springfield, Mass.,	96	91
Worcester,	99	86
Providence,	92	94
Boston,	93	91
Totals,	2327	2163

Average: Carver, 93. Bogardus, 86.

This shows an extraordinary high score, but it was not stated at what elevation the birds were thrown. It is, however, currently reported *on the road*, that after the *first few shoots*, in which some indifferent scores were made, that the traps were changed for others with *weaker springs*, and that the birds were thrown at a very great elevation for a good high record.

I have no desire to depreciate the performance of anyone, but would rather prefer to give more credit that was due, but feel obliged to take cognizance of statements made to me by men of integrity and ability. It is certainly remarkable that the scores in the latter part of the series were very different from the earlier ones. The Ligowsky Co. are very reticent, and appear *to know nothing*, or prefer, anyhow, *to say nothing;* but time will tell if the form shown in exhibitions by celebrated shots will be maintained in contests where the traps are handled by *independent parties* and set properly.

Captain E. E. Stubbs and Gwynne Price have competed in eight exhibition matches, attempting to beat the records in the Carver-Bogardus contests. Conditions were the same, except at Logansport, where some trees interfered, the birds were never thrown higher than 25 feet at 40 yards; one of the matches was at 21 and one at 25 yards rise.

	STUBBS.	PRICE.
Paragould, Ark.,	93	87
Decatur, Ill.,	99	89
Logansport, Ind.,	100	97
Fort Wayne, Ind.,	96	88
Pittsburg,	88	88
"	89	86
"	100	92
"	99	93
Totals,	764	720

Average: Stubbs, 95. Gwynne Price, 90.

The most extraordinary score recorded was that made by Captain Stubbs at a *semi-private Press Exhibition*, at the Madison Square Garden, New York City. With a 12 bore, $7\frac{1}{2}$ lb. Greener Gun and American Wood Powder, $1\frac{1}{4}$ oz. No. 8

Chilled Shot, he broke five clays straight, at 45 yards rise, one barrel, all broken at over 60 yards. He also scored 30 in succession, at 25 yards rise, using second barrel twice only.

In a match at Pittsburg, *21 yards rise*, 75 birds each, Stubbs scored 73, Price 69.

It will be noticed that the scores of Stubbs and Price, in their eight shoots, are 193 *ahead* of the first eight of the Carver-Bogardus contests.

Both Captain Stubbs and Gwynne Price shot with 10 bore, 9 lb. guns, made expressly for them by W. W. Greener, and often birds at 35 and 40 yards were shattered *into mere smoke*, no fragments being visible.

At Pittsburg, Captain Stubbs scored 150 without a miss, with one of the Westley Richards' 10 bore guns; and Gwynne Price broke 67 straight with a 12 bore, 8 lb. gun, of the Pittsburg Fire Arms Co.'s make.

Some very fine shooting has been made by Mr. Bell, of Pittsburg, a splendid shot, and an extraordinary performance is copied from the Nashville *American* into the *American Field*, of Mr. Andy Meaders, of Nashville, who is said to have broken 97 in 100, the other 3 also hit, at 18 yards rise, 4 traps, 4th notch, using *one hand* only. Mr. S. A. Tucker was said to have been present. Feeling a little dubious of the accuracy of this statement, I wrote to Mr. Meaders for confirmation of the account, but as he did not condescend even the *courtesy of a reply* to my letter, it more than ever convinces me that there is a reason for his silence.

I just hear that Captain Stubbs has, in a private trial, broken 395 clays in 500, at 15 yards rise, 3rd notch, with a *Kennedy Rifle*, using *full regulation* factory cartridges, breaking 92 in the *last* 100.

LOADING.

The subject of loading has been of late so well ventilated in the sporting press, that it is scarcely necessary to refer to it, but that every one seems to have a *hobby of his own*, or some *specialty* to recommend; I propose simply to give my own experience, based upon the opinion, that as a maximum charge of $1\frac{1}{4}$ oz. of shot is allowed in *most* contests, it is advisable to load so that your gun will do the best execution with that charge, for common sense dictates that the more shot you can use without sacrifice of penetration, the better.

Guns of 10 and 12 bore will be used by every man of discrimination and judgment, and my advice is to load with $1\frac{1}{4}$ oz. of 7 or 8 chilled shot, and by careful experiments find out the *heaviest charge of powder* that each particular gun will shoot that quantity of shot *without loss of pattern*, by which means the best chances of success will be assured.

By using chilled shot a greater number of pellets can be had so that full measure of Dixon's 1106 can be used for same weight. Greater penetration will also be made. A small quantity of antimony with the lead in chilled shot is said to make the shot harder and lighter.

Ordinarily a 10 bore gun, weighing 9 or 10 lbs., will shoot $4\frac{1}{2}$ to $5\frac{1}{2}$ drams of powder; and a 12 bore gun $3\frac{1}{2}$ to 5 drams of powder, if 8 lbs. to 9 lbs. weight. I saw some good work done recently with a 10 bore, 11 pound gun, with 8 drams of powder; but I am in favor of restricting guns in matches to not exceeding *10 lbs. and 10 bore;* and I would allow 2 yards distance to 12 bore guns if using *only* 1 1-8 of shot.

In double barrel shooting, the advantage of using the American Wood powder at all events *in the first barrel*, is so obvious that it is almost unnecessary to refer to it, except for the few who may not have seen it.

Some good judges and prominent shots will insist that the Wood powder is *slower* than the black, and therefore they use as a primer, about half a dram of the black powder. Out of deference to those opinions, I have used it so loaded sometimes, but have failed to realize the advantages. Certainly most of the best scores I have made and seen, were with the Wood powder, pure and simple; and even a small quantity of black must, in some degree, produce smoke and fouling.

With the Wood powder I should not wipe out my gun in a match at 100 birds, but always *blow through the barrels* after each shot, and occasionally dip the muzzle in water. There is an indescribable sort of greasiness in using Wood powder which, keeping the barrel moist, prevents caking.

As was the case with the original yellow Dittmar, so with the Wood powder; it requires great confinement by ramming and wadding, and the agents for it, Von Lengerke & Detmold, of New York, who have had great experience with it, give explicit directions for its proper use. Mr. Von Lengerke, a practical man and one of the best amateur shots in the country, has made some wonderful shooting with the Wood powder in public contests; and I strongly advise my readers to try a few shells loaded by his firm if they wish to give the powder a fair trial.

There is no saving in using cheap powder or wads, and the best way I find, is to use a dry Baldwin wad and one of the thick felt or two pink edge wads on powder. A thin wad is sufficient on shot with a crimped paper shell; but if brass shells I advise a thin paper wad and then a Baldwin wad upside down, which, presenting a rough edge upwards, will prevent the wad starting. I have seldom found the shot loosen when loaded in this way; but as a precaution in using brass shells, it is well, whenever the first barrel only is fired, to change the shell from second barrel into the first for next shot, and in doing so observe that the wad is firm on shot, and if not, press it down with the thumb. Brass shells should always be carried shot upwards in the belt.

Wads should be firmly pressed down, and if Wood powder, should be tapped with a mallet, using an extra wad over powder if length of shell will admit. It must not be hammered so as to bulge the shell, but the more the powder is confined by close fitting wads, the better will be the shooting.

For clay pigeon shooting, I prefer fine grain powder as being quickest, and No. 8 chilled shot at 18 yards rise, with an ordinary cylinder or moderately choked gun, but with an exceptionally close shooting gun No. 7, or even No. 6 shot, may perhaps answer well; but as a rule, I think, as the clay pigeon is now made, No. 8 shot is heavy enough.

I have noticed many inquiries in the *Sporting Press* as to the best method of removing lead and caking from gun barrels. Choke bore guns are most particularly liable to this very serious impediment to good shooting, getting caked at muzzle as well as breech, which is solely caused by the saltpetre in the powder.

It is claimed that washing out with rag and coal oil will remove it, but it is a great mistake, for oil has little effect upon saltpetre; but if the barrels are put breech downward in a pail and plenty of boiling water poured into them until very heated, a brush or rag will clear it away instantly with the gun rod.

The Wood powder does not foul in the same manner, because it is free from saltpetre; and out in the field or where hot water is not obtainable, a few shots with the Wood powder occasionally, will clear away the fouling.

I made over 600 shots in exhibition matches at Pittsburg, using Wood powder, and never wiped out the barrels, which did not appear more foul than after the first shot; occasionally the muzzle was dipped in water to cool the barrels.

Some prominent shots go as far as to assert that certain guns will shoot one size of shot better than another. I do not believe in it until it comes to the large sizes, where, undoubtedly, it is better for it to chamber properly. Let them, however, ride that hobby or any other that will inspire confidence if for nothing else, for in public shooting especially, a stock of it is an advantage.

In illustration of this I may mention an experience of my own: About 10 years since I was contending in an optional sweepstake, 50 or 100 dollars each, at the Junior Gun Club, London, England. The first prize was a gold cup, value 500 dollars and cash 350 dollars; 150 dollars to second and 100 to third; 25 pigeons each, at 25 yards rise first day, and 25 at 30 yards rise second day.

Previously to this time I had contended in many sweepstakes where the first prize was 500 dollars and upwards at equal distances, and I had succeeded in winning every one. In the first days' shooting I stood second with a score of 19; and as the man ahead of me was not considered equal to myself at 30 yards, I thought, bar accident, that I must win.

The maker of my gun, who was present, and felt interested in my chance of winning, had been observing my shooting critically, and thinking that the gun was scattering a little, asked me to allow him to take it to the workshop, make a little alteration and return it in the morning.

The next day he insisted upon my seeing it targetted before the match, as he had much improved it; when much to my disgust, it was anything but what it should have been. The consequence was that *I lost all confidence*, and it undoubtedly cost me the loss of the stake also, for I made a very poor score; and ever since I have made up my mind to "let well alone" and allow others to try experiments.

The system of handicapping is the only true method of giving a moderate shot a chance of winning, and is becoming general in really first-class clubs. It is fully described in a separate chapter further on; but in clay pigeon shooting, the distance should range from 12 to 25 yards, which will be sufficient difference to bring the best and worst upon a level; whereas class shooting is simply "a delusion and a snare"—a very nice arrangement of the clever few to induce an inferior shot to believe that he can hold his own against them. A careful reading of the remarks on that subject will convince them of the absurdity of such ideas.

Sportsmen, fond of field pursuits, seem naturally to feel a pleasure in taking life, consequently the shooting of live pigeons will to some extent be kept up; but when we find that at most gatherings it is not once in ten times that anything approaching to good flying birds are supplied, and that even then they are six times at least more cost than the clay; that the expense of handling and trouble of feeding is dispensed with; and also the great uncertainty of the supply either of tame or wild birds—it is to be expected that in a year or two the clay will supersede the live bird shooting.

No exception can be taken to the clays by the most fastidious on the plea of cruelty or inhumanity, and one of the greatest arguments in its favor is, that perfect equality in the birds is certain for each competitor, there being no incomers or non-flyers.

It may not be the case to so great extent in Europe, and more especially in England, for although the birds may not be of a better breed, and no wild birds are to be got, still they are supplied in better condition and properly handled and trapped, so that seldom more than two or three in a hundred are refused for hanging on traps.

The example of that first-class club, the Audubon, of Chicago, in using the ground traps only, will be sure to be followed; and the safest way to ensure having good birds is to refuse and not pay for, those unable to fly; and the dealer will soon see the necessity of paying more attention to the condition of pigeons, and being satisfied with a little less profit than the exorbitant price now demanded gives them.

This trouble with the birds has caused such a revulsion of feeling in favor of a good substitute, that in a few years perhaps, the stock of both wild and tame birds may be so increased that the price will be reduced and some good sport from ground traps be had. No one more than myself will be pleased to see it.

In clay pigeon shooting, as the object is so much smaller than the body of a pigeon, it is a necessity to have a gun that not only shoots very closely, but also makes a very regular pattern, and the ammunition and loading should be of the best. The object should be struck with the centre of the charge, for although it may have been hit on the edge with one or two pellets from the outer circle of the charge, which from collision have lost power, it may not be broken so as to be scored. The shooter then stands in the same position, as is very often the case when a live birds is wounded and manages to struggle over the boundary line. I am satisfied that in nearly every instance, when the clay pigeon is hit and not broken, that it is more the fault of the shooter than anything else.

Shooting from three or five traps is particularly to be advocated, as where only one trap is used, and the trapper has to alter the flight and elevation for each shot, however careful he may be, there will be "kickers" ready to find fault if they miss a bird, and some are continually charging the trapper or puller with intentional favoritism.

Where more than one trap is used no alteration is required, and if the instructions in my rules are carefully carried out, the most perfect equality of chances will be found for every shooter; for by using a die as directed, an equal quantity of straight-away and quartering shots will be had. In double bird shooting, by using the centre trap every time and one of the others, it will produce good practice and perfect equality; and the birds must rise together if both strings are pulled by one hand.

I fail to see any necessity for screens behind the traps, it spoils the appearance of the grounds and looks so much like a circus performance; for with a lively puller and good traps three or five yards apart, there will not be many birds shot at nearer than 50 feet from the traps. Great precaution is necessary that the shooter cannot know the traps to be pulled, which can be done by placing the puller behind the level of the shooter, and having the strings where handled hidden by a screen of some kind between shooter and puller.

No more particular instruction is necessary in shooting clay pigeons that would be required with live birds from a ground trap, if the clay is thrown at a proper elevation, but not half so much allowance need be made in either rising or falling shots as with glass balls. If the clay is thrown at an improperly high elevation, it meets the wind more fully, and consequently travels more slowly and is soon exhausted; such practice requires very little skill, and is harmful, for it is no better than a sitting shot.

Just before the clay falls it is almost stationary and presents a very easy shot, but it is generally at so great a distance that the shot having spread very much, it is not easily scored. It also falls more slowly than a glass ball, and requires very little undershooting, for the glass ball being circular and smaller falls very quickly and requires a considerable allowance.

The principal difference between the clay and live pigeon, which must be carefully kept in view, is, that whereas the speed of the clay is greatest on leaving the trap and decreases very considerable after about 25 yards; the live bird travels faster the further it goes until well out of danger. This is of great importance to observe when shooting with the use of both barrels, because where it is necessary to shoot well ahead of a live bird if at all quartering, at a distance of 45 or 50 yards, the clay at the same place would be well nigh exhausted, and the aim then should be almost *dead on*.

Every bird should be shot at within 15 yards, or certainly not over 20 yards from the trap, or the shot may have spread too much to make a dead certainty of breaking the clay, more particularly if large sized shot is used. It is better to strike the object with three small sized shot and take chances of breaking it than to run the risk of missing it altogether; small sized shot therefore is preferable, unless the gun shoots *exceptionally* close.

I have mentioned in another part of this book that the greatest secrect in wing shooting is, "never allow your gun to be brought upon a bird from above or before it, but always from behind if cross shots, or below if rising shots." I will add here: Never, under any circumstance in wing shooting, let the motion of the gun meet the object, but follow the exact line of the bird until sufficiently in front, and from above if falling shots, in which case a very small allowance should be made, as mentioned before at a falling clay.

The most difficult of all shots is a slightly rising and also slightly quartering bird, as two awkward motions have to be provided for at the same time; and in making the one it very often happens that a failure is made to exactly meet the other. In clays more especially, the rapidity of the flight for the first 20 yards necessitates aiming well ahead in quartering shots, particularly so with right quarterers, as referred to more fully further on in this book under a special diagram. Take care also to keep your gun very firmly held in the hand, and perfectly level.

In a few private trials and nine public matches, I have gained the experience before mentioned. The result of the nine exhibition shoots, in which I shot at 875 clays, at various distances from 18 to 25 yards rise, 789 were scored. I made the most miserable failure in the two first private trials, until I fully realized the terrific pace at which the clays leave the trap, after which I made very good scores, and soon began to like the clay practice better than any I have ever had at live birds in this country.

The plan I have suggested in rule 20, for signaling the result of each shot, will be found of great utility in large assemblies, saving much labor by giving notice in all parts of the ground almost instantaneously and with the greatest accuracy, whether a kill or a miss has to be scored.

The introduction of the clay pigeon will be the means of ridding trap-shooting of its most objectionable elements, particularly those most relied upon by the fastidious humanitarians, cruelty and danger. The way to prevent further legislation to stop the shooting of live birds from the trap, is to have every bird gathered and killed before another is shot at, as this alone stayed the passing of a bill in the English Legislature, for no cruelty could be proved, more than was constantly occurring in field shooting.

No outside shooting or scouting should, under any circumstances, be tolerated, as more danger arises from outsiders shooting at wounded birds in the direction of the crowd round the shooters, than from the contestants, whose arms are only loaded at the mark.

It is also urged that it is an unnecessary and wanton sacrifice of life for the purpose of sport, which is indeed farfetched, being nothing more than the killing of the birds for food, as in ordinary hunting and fishing.

The question of danger does not arise in clay pigeon shooting at all, as the birds are thrown within a prescribed limit, none being turned toward the shooters, and no scouting need be apprehended.

There is no luck or chances of good or bad birds, so often the cause of dissatisfaction in live bird shooting, as the most perfect fairness and equality may be relied upon when the traps are handled with knowledge and care; and a straight-away bird will be found as difficult as any, or perhaps even more so.

A serious drawback to glass ball shooting has been the broken fragments of glass on lawns, shooting grounds and base ball parks; whereas, with the clays a frost and a rain will cause the broken pieces to dissolve into dust.

Some ladies feel great pleasure in hunting and fishiug excursions, and have no objection to seeing game killed in a legitimate manner, because wherever wounded it is gathered and killed at once, without lengthened and unnecessary suffering. Some even join in the pursuit of game in the field, and there is no reason whatever why ladies of refined and cultured taste should not contest in games of skill with the rifle and shot gun, with the same spirit of rivalry, as they do now with the long bow at Archery Tournaments. Not a shadow of a pretext can be urged against it, and it is certain that the presence of ladies on a shooting ground will command the greatest propriety; and if the interest of the fair sex can be enlisted in this direction, there is no reason why shooting tournaments will not soon take the lead as *the* national amusement.

CLASS SHOOTING.

A few remarks on quite recent experience in class shooting. Eight shooters competed for a stake of 5 dollars each, 6 birds, class shooting. Six made a clear score of 6 each and divided first money, about 3½ dollars each; one killed one only and received second, 12 dollars; and one missed all and took third prize, 8 dollars. Now if one of those who killed all, had intentionally missed one bird he would have gotten the 12 dollars, and if another had missed two he also would have secured 8 dollars by a fraud; but as each shot honestly and did his best, they only got back a little more than half the entrance money; whereas, two shooters without a particle of a pretension to skill, took the most money in second and third prizes.

This reminds one forcibly of donkey racing, where each jockey rides an opponent's donkey, and the one coming in last gets the race. Can absurdity be more absurd?

I also saw at the same meeting a case which shows how sometimes a fraud, unintentionally committed, works an injustice upon outside parties. In a stake of 15 entries, same conditions as mentioned above, the result was as follows:

A,	111111	F,	111110	K,	010111
B,	111111	G,	110101	L,	010111
C,	111111	H,	001111	M,	001111
D,	111111	I,	011101	N,	110010
E,	111111	J,	001111	O,	110000

A casual glance at the score will show that at the 6th round F, who was an old hand at the game, could see by carefully watching the score, that if he killed his bird he would be in a hot corner with five good shots to shoot off for first money; or, if he divided he would barely save his entrance fee, but if he intentionally missed the bird he must take the second money with a score of five, as all the others had missed two or more; so he had only to let his gun *jar off*, or, in other words, to do a robbery, and he pocketed 22½ dollars.

Now, the worst has to come. There was considerable betting and pool selling on the match, and F, who was known to be a gentleman and a fine shot, had been freely backed to win first money; and his feelings can be imagined when he was informed that his most intimate friend and companion had lost a very considerable sum of money in betting on the result, having backed him to win. If he had thought of the injury he was causing to innocent and confiding parties, he would not have been guilty of such a fraudulent act, and he was exceedingly sorry for it afterwards.

At the same tournament I saw several birds dead when thrown from the traps, and if the shooters had fired when the dead body was in the air, they would have had a dead bird scored to them.

I had the pleasure of meeting there several ardent lovers of trap shooting, who were aware of my efforts to make the sport what it ought to be; but they said they all desired a radical change, and they felt sure that it must come in a short time, as soon as the majority of shooters had their attention drawn to the subject of class shooting.

English Style Holding Gun. American Style Holding Gun.
Five Ground Traps. Plunge Trap.

Selected Opinions of the Press

ON THE

Clay Pigeon.

[From *Forest and Stream*, New York.]

"* * * This flight so nearly resembles the actual motion of the birds, that the Clay Pigeons afford excellent practice for wing shooting. We commend all sportsmen to test its merits."

[From *American Field*, New York and Chicago.]

"* * * We feel warranted in saying that the use of this new invention will largely fill the void in trap-shooting made by the scarcity of the wild pigeon."

[From *Turf, Field and Farm*, New York.]

"The flight of the projectile—which is saucer shaped—is much like that of the quail, and therefore preferable to glass balls for practice. As the clay "birds" soon become broken and mingled with the dirt, no damage can ensue, as is often the case with broken glass balls."

[From *The Field*, London, England.]

"This appears to us to be the best plan hitherto brought out of affording the tyro a cheap method of learning to shoot either in public or private."

[From *The Illustrated London News*, London, England.]

"It is immensely superior to the gyro pigeon, or any other substitute for the live bird, and is sure to meet with great favor from those who wish to become good game shots."

[*Bogardus Says.*]

"Clay pigeons are by far a superior article for the sportsman, the use of which perfects one rapidly as a wing shot."

SEND FOR CIRCULARS TO

THE LIGOWSKY CLAY PIGEON CO.,

P. O. Box 1292.   CINCINNATI, OHIO, U. S. A.

RULES

FOR

CLAY PIGEON SHOOTING

FROM

ONE, THREE AND FIVE TRAPS.

BY

GWYNNE PRICE,

St. Louis, Mo.

RULE 1. *Referee.* The referee having been accepted by the contestants, his decision upon all questions shall be *absolutely final.* He shall, however, be allowed to ask the opinion of two or three *disinterested* spectators before giving his decision, if he has a reasonable doubt.

RULE 2. *Traps.* The traps shall be set in a line or semicircle, numbered left to right, at *an agreed notch*, and to throw the birds at *not greater* than an elevation of 20 feet at 40 yards from the traps. A screen may be placed behind each trap, and a 15 yards circle shall be marked by stakes in front of the traps.

RULE 3. *One Trap.* The elevation and horizontal flight of the birds shall be fairly changed by trapper for each shot.

RULE 4. *Three Traps.* The traps shall be set 6 yards apart. The centre trap in front of the shooter, shall be set to throw *straight-away* birds. The No. 1 trap to throw *right half-quarterers*, and the No. 3 trap *left half-quarterers*. On the die, 1 and 2 shall denote the No. 1 trap; Nos. 3 and 4, trap No. 2; Nos. 5 and 6, No. 3 trap.

RULE 5. *Five Traps.* The traps shall be set 4 yards apart. Nos. 1 and 4 to throw *right half-quarterers;* Nos. 2 and 5 to throw *left half-quarterers*, and No. 3, *drivers.* On the die, Nos. 3 and 6 shall denote *centre* trap; to secure equal chances for quartering and driving shots.

RULE 6. *Double Rises.* The centre trap shall be used every shot—the second trap decided by wads 1, 2, 4 and 5, or die, Nos. 3 and 6 not being counted. Both strings shall be pulled with *one hand only.* The distances shall be 3 yards nearer than single rises. Both birds shall be scored if broken by one shot. If either bird falls within the 15 yards, the shooter may, at his option, claim another *full rise.*

RULE 7. *Entry.* No entry can be made after the *first bird* in the *second round* has been shot at, unless the person shall have arrived *too late* to enter at proper time; in which case an entry may be made up to the *end of second round*, by consent of majority of the contestants. More than one chance may be taken if no added money or prize is *given.* Absence of more than five minutes will entail disqualification, unless Referee should allow it as excusable.

RULE 8. *Pulling.* When the shooter calls "Pull," the trap shall be *instantly* sprung, or the bird may be refused. If pulled without notice, or more than one bird is loosed, if the shooter fires, he must abide by the consequences. If he fails to shoot when the trap is *properly pulled*, it must be scored a *lost bird.*

RULE 9. *Distance.* The rise shall be 15 or 18 yards for single and 12 or 15 yards for double rises, or by a handicap of 12 to 25 yards *according to merit.* If a contestant shoots at less than the proper distance he shall have another bird if he kills, but if he misses it shall be scored lost. A winner or divider of 10 dollars or more shall go back one yard for every such win *during that day*, and if he is standing at the 25 yards limit, all the others shall *go in one yard.*

RULE 10. *Gun size.* Breech-loading guns *only* shall be allowed, not larger than 10 bore and 10 pounds in weight. Guns of 12 bore and less allowed 2 yards if using 1 1-8 oz. shot.

Rule 11 *Gun holding.* The Referee shall see that the gun is held fairly *below the shoulder, inside* or *in front of* the arm until the shooter calls *"Pull."* If this rule is infringed and the bird is killed the Referee shall order another bird shot at.

Rule 12. *Gun loading.* Charge of powder *unlimited.* Shot shall not exceed 1 1-4 ounce, Dixon's measure, 1106 for 10 bore guns, or 1 1-8 for 12 bore and under. No concentrators or other substance than powder, shot and wads allowed.

Rule 13. *Challenge.* Contestants only may, after depositing 5 dollars, request the Referee to examine the loading of a shooter as he goes to the score. If the charge is proper, the shooter shall receive the 5 dollars deposited; but if illegal, he shall be disqualified.

Rule 14. *Danger.* If a bird is thrown so that to shoot *in proper time* would endanger life or property, the Referee shall, if requested, allow another bird whether the gun was fired or not. Closing a gun *before going to the score*, or failing to open it *before leaving the mark*, will subject shooter to penalty of one dollar.

Rule 15. *Miss-fire, etc..* If a miss-fire occur through any fault of shooter, it shall be a *lost bird;* but if gun was properly loaded and cocked, it shall be a *no bird*, at shooter's cost. If the second barrel miss-fire, another bird shall be allowed, and the first barrel fired *properly at the bird*, but with *powder only*, except in double rise shooting; if first barrel miss-fire and the second be used, the bird shall be scored. If two barrels are fired at same time and the bird killed, another bird shall be shot at, but if missed it shall be a *lost bird.*

Rule 16. *Shot marks. No* bird shall be examined for *shot marks*, but shall be scored *lost* unless the Referee sees it distinctly broken in the air. If he has any doubt he may either order *another bird* or *refer for opinions*, as per Rule 1.

Rule 17. *Bird imperfect.* If a bird is broken by the trap it shall in any case be a *no bird*, unless the handle only shall be left in the trap. If a bird falls within the 15 yards circle, if broken, it shall be scored; but if missed, it shall be a *no bird.*

RULE 18. *Division.* Stakes shall be divided into three prizes, of 50, 30 and 20 per cent., after deducting cost of birds, for the *three best shots.* If an entry of 20 or more shooters, into four prizes, of 40, 30, 20 and 10 per cent. *All tie birds* to be deducted from full money before division.

RULE 19. *Ties.* If a tie in a private match, the bet is off. All other ties shall be shot off at *same time, same number* of birds and *conditions,* unless a majority should agree otherwise, and shoot *miss and out,* or divide. If a postponement should take place, *from any cause,* any contestant may depute *another in the ties* to shoot for him, if it is not convenient to attend again.

RULE 20. *Signaling score.* The Referee shall have two flags, *red* and *white.* If a kill, he shall raise the *red* flag; if a miss, the *white* flag. In *double rises* the *red* flag denotes *two kills,* the *white* flag *two misses;* a *kill* and a *miss* the red flag *above* white; a miss and a kill, the white flag *above* red. A *no-bird,* both flags *down.*

RULE 21. *Fines.* A fine of one dollar shall be strictly charged for: *Use of bad language.—Ungentlemanly conduct.—Incautious handling of firearms.—Interference with shooter at score.—Remarks intended to influence decision of Referee,*—and *Insulting behavior to any person on the ground.*

THE GUN,

AND HOW TO USE IT TO KILL EVERY FAIR WING SHOT.

Very few persons using the shot-gun that I have met with, seem to attach sufficient importance to the requirements necessary to make good wing practice, as their attention has not been drawn to the absolute necessity of carefully studying the allowance to be made in shooting for *distance, flight, windage, pace* and *position*, whether *under* or *over* the level of the gun, etc., etc.

It is generally thought that in order to ensure a kill you should be *dead on* the object; but no greater mistake can be made, for unless your bird is going straight away and on the same level as yourself, to be *dead on* really means *to be dead off.*

My attention was never drawn so particularly to this subject until I began to shoot pigeons from a ground-trap. The birds if really good, generally fly very low, and it could easily be observed whether the shot struck *above, below, right* or *left* of the mark; and as I shoot with both eyes open, I could see what was the reason if I missed, and it required very little common sense to adopt a remedy.

The handling of a gun is to be compared only to the delicate manipulation of the strings or keys of a musical instrument, and can only be acquired artistically by those who are almost *born to it.*

The earlier a gun is placed in the hands of a youth, the more likely is he to become expert, and such a proficient in the art of shooting, as to feel the extraordinary sensations of pleasure experienced *only* by those who are able to excel in any profession they engage in.

As a rule the sportsman whose ordinary calling is of a light and delicate nature, is most likely to use his gun elegantly; but it does not at all follow that he possesses the steady nerve so essential to a good shot.

It is very easy to give instruction and advice on marksmanship; but there are times when the very best shots fail in carrying out the system which they well know is requisite, and often shoot impulsively without being able to prevent it, well aware before the trigger is pulled that they will be sure to miss the object.

Pigeon shooting from the trap is most excellent practice for a beginner, after he can handle his gun easily, particularly if he shoots before a crowd of people, as it steadies his nerves, and he can observe how the more accomplished gunners perform; but it is rather expensive amusement if indulged in often. Glass-ball shooting costs very little; care should, however, be used in selecting the trap throwing the ball most like the flight of a bird.

Many fine game shots are at first very deficient at the trap, simply because they are nervous in company; but I never yet saw a good trap shot that could not do fair execution in the field after very little experience.

My readers must not suppose that I do not miss many shots; but when I do, I am always ready to admit that it was my own fault, and not from a defect in the gun; although I often hear shooters declare if they have missed, that they were *dead on* their bird, when I have noticed the shot was awfully wide of the mark, and they are ever ready with an excuse, blaming either the maker of their gun, or the quality of the powder.

It is far easier, I candidly confess, to preach than to practice; and I would say to my friends in the language of a Clergyman in the old country, not possessed of a particularly high moral character:

"*Do as I say, not as I do.*"

Always use the very best of ammunition, powder and wads more especially; the extra game killed will far more than compensate for the difference in cost—but remember use plenty of powder.

A 10 bore gun will take 5 drams of powder and $1\frac{1}{4}$ oz. of shot, without recoil; and a 12 bore 4 drams of powder and $1\frac{1}{8}$ oz. of shot, if of 9 or 10 lbs. weight, and held firmly in the hand. If your gun rebound unpleasantly, reduce the charge of shot a little.

Soft felt wads will be found best for muzzle-loading guns, as they are more easily rammed down when the barrel becomes foul.

I would most emphatically impress upon all young shots that with a moderately good gun a few yards in distance is of little consequence, and that it is far better to wait until you can get proper aim, than to fire random shots.

A stray pellet may occasionally kill, but there is so much space around a small bird that it is quite twenty chances to one against killing, unless you are in the right direction, especially with a choke bore gun.

When a covey of birds rise together, the greatest quickness combined with steadiness is requisite, so as to select the two most advantageous chances.

Never shoot wildly into them, or you may wound several without killing any. Each bird should be shot at as carefully as though only one was on the wing.

If in company, you will, of course, select your birds from those on your own side, and your companion will take the like precaution. Be sure take the bird farthest from you for the first barrel, or it may be out of distance for your second, unless you are wonderfully quick, and it is a great saving of time and trouble to get two birds at one rise.

Many times in my youthful days I have shot a couple of charges into a covey of 18 or 20 partridges, apparently so close together on the wing that a horse rug would have covered the lot, and not a bird have I killed.

No game should if practicable ever be shot at a less distance than 25 yards, and even then it will be almost useless for the table if the gun shoots closely. It is much better to wait, as at 35 yards the shot will cover a much larger space.

It is a very bad habit to shoot at any object sitting, after having once accustomed yourself to wing practice. It will be found much easier to kill flying shots, as the body is more exposed when the wings are extended, and the bird presents nearly twice the size.

Occasionally it may be necessary to shoot game when perched, or on the ground, and in doing so it will be best to level the gun *below* the mark, and steadily elevate it until the line is a little over the object, as the muzzle is likely to be lowered rather than raised in the action of pulling the trigger; although most guns being thickest at the breech and the rib highest at back, they will throw the shot rather over the direct line. A shooter will soon find what his gun does.

When a bird rises, the eye or eyes, *for some of the best shots keep both open*, should be steadily observing and following *the exact course of flight;* the hands should act in the most perfect harmony with the eye and the will, and the gun will come to the eye instinctively. It must be brought up a little behind the object, and the motion increased until the sight is well in front, and the trigger pulled without the movement of the gun being stayed *in the slightest degree*. The firmer the gun is held with both hands, the better, *with the left hand well forward*, so as to keep the exact position, and the less recoil will be felt. *(See front cover.)*

Should the bird be in front considerably over your level, take the sight a little underneath, and the bird will fly into the line of the shot. If going right or left follow the exact course until well ahead before firing. The farther off it is, and the swifter the flight, the greater allowance must there be made. For instance if at 20 or 25 yards, just in front of the bird's head will be sufficient, if the motion of the gun is kept slightly increasing, whereas if the object be 50 or 60 yards away and *flying swiftly*, in some cases two or even three feet ahead will not be too much, depending entirely upon circumstances of which the gunner himself will be the best judge, after a little careful consideration.

When I say three or four feet, I mean what would appear three or four feet at 60 yards, because an object four fcet long at 60 yards does not appear over three feet, so that when shooting three feet ahead of a quartering fast flying bird at 60 yards, you are really aiming between four and five feet in front of it.

In order to become a good judge of distance, measure out say 30, 40, 50 and 60 yards at your own homestead, and often study it.

I have heard shooters say: "*What a long shot, why that was 70 yards;*" when upon stepping it out, it was not really 50.

The *pull of the trigger*, the *quickness of the powder*, of which the small grain is said to be the best for snap shots, (although perhaps not quite so strong) have all to be considered, bearing in mind that three-fourths, if not more of the shots missed, are from being behind rather than in front.

This remember and treasure up, as the greatest secret in shooting: *Never allow your gun to be brought upon a bird from above, or before it; but always from behind if cross shots, or below if rising shots. The course of flight being in direct opposition to the motion of the gun, unless that instruction is followed, it would require at least double allowance to be made, and even then I very much question unless in very experienced hands, whether one shot in twenty would be effective.*

Two opposing motions in machinery produce awful consequences; and in the same degree in gunnery, it is hardly possible to calculate the effect of the flight of a bird being opposed to the movement of the gun.

The greatest care should also be used that the gun is held level, so that the line from the eye in taking sight should be along the *centre of the rib*, from the screw at breech to the sight on muzzle. (See addenda, page 26.)

With ground game the same principle applies more or less, remembering that whereas with birds *above* your level going *right away*, you shoot under them; hares or rabbits and even birds near the ground being *below* your level, it is requisite to be well over them, carefully calculating whether it is rising or falling ground, and with side shots be well in front as explained before.

If a hare or rabbit is crossing you in brush or timber, and you only just get a sight, snap shoot three or four feet in front of where you saw it, and you will be almost sure to find that you have killed. So with a wood-cock, shoot after him in the direction he was taking, although you have lost sight, for being a very soft bird, a single pellet may kill him at 50 or 60 yards. It will be found to answer very often.

I have observed that in the field and also at the trap, many good shots miss a larger proportion of right quartering birds than when going to the left.

Several reasons suggest themselves. The shooter stands with his left foot forward, consequently it is easier for him to turn to the left than to the right, more especially with a corpulent person.

Again, the left hand being held most forward along the barrel, it has greater command of the gun than the trigger hand; and the pressure of the finger in pulling the trigger is very apt to stay the motion of the gun in right hand shots.

You scarcely ever see a missed right hand bird, but which is lost from shooting behind it.

In trap shooting, I think it well to cover the No. 4 trap, instead of No. 3; it is as easy to wheel 15 yards to the left, as it is 5 yards to the right. Hold the gun firmly, and shoot more forward at the right quartering birds than others. Remember this particularly, that with side birds, there is lots of time to get good, certain aim, before firing, for the bird is not getting further from you as he would if going straight away, and a quartering bird is the easiest shot possible, with proper care and steadiness.

Since writing the above, a remarkable confirmation of this occurred in the Bogardus-Hauworth plunge trap match, at St. Louis. Bogardus was one bird ahead at the ninety-eighth round, and offered $100 to a dollar that he would win the match. Both having killed in the next round, and Hauworth in front having killed his bird, Bogardus had to score his last bird to win. He got a very fast bird, well up in the air, half quartering to the right and *fast rising;* just the most difficult of all shots to kill; and although being at 21 yards rise, he took plenty of time, but shooting as would be most likely the case, slightly behind the bird, although striking him with one or two shots through the rump, being favored by the wind he carried it right over, and lost Bogardus the match, the result being a tie of 92. It was somewhat singular also that Bogardus killed 21 left quartering birds, but missed three right quarterers, and Hauworth killed 21 left quarterers, but missed four to the right, neither having missed a left hand shot.

The more trouble bestowed upon these little matters the better; and the best judge of *distance* and *pace* will be the most successful in making a good bag.

I have generally found that the fastest flying birds are, the duck, teal, and some quail.

The snipe and prairie chicken fly swiftly when with a strong wind; but snipe, if hunted *down* wind, which they always should be, will generally turn *against* it; and then they present the very easiest side shots of any bird I have ever met with.

Most young sportsmen are afraid to hunt jack snipe, because they have been told it is a difficult bird to kill. Generally they are found in the open, and although they *wobble* about a good deal when they first rise, let them get 15 or 20 yards on the wing, then they fly as straight and as steadily as any bird I know, and are very easily killed.

There is very little good snipe shooting in England, and one of the small sized Wilson snipe, which, by the bye, I have never met with in this country, is almost as great a rarity as a black swan. It is a much more difficult bird to kill, than the full sized jack seen here, and I well recollect when a boy, my father who was a fair shot at general game, having 8 double shots at one bird, and at last he got a chance and finished him sitting.

Before I had scarcely any practice at snipe, I heard Bogardus say when he was in Wales, the first time he was over in

England, that he would back himself to kill 100 snipe in succession and take every fair shot.

It appeared to me that it was about 100 to 1 against his doing it, but after I arrived in this country, I had the pleasure of seeing him kill them right and left at 40, 50 and 60 yards, and about as easily as he now breaks the glass balls. It gave me confidence in hunting with him, and since then I have mightily enjoyed hunting snipe, and I killed 103 the last I ever shot at.

Every young beginner should hunt snipe; it is splendid sport, with good retrieving pointers; and even the common meadow lark is really good practice in the summer season.

The quail is by many thought a very easy bird to kill; but I think the hunter who will score 7 out of 10 the day through in central Illinois, where it is mostly corn and ragweed shooting, can hold his own in any company, and at any game.

I met with two bevies of quail, on the estate of John Gillett, Esq., near Elkhart, Logan Co., Illinois, that were the swiftest flying birds I ever saw, I scattered them in corn about eight feet high, and had eleven shots at one lot before I scored one; and I never took the trouble to look for either again, but left them for breeding; as about half a dozen of any of that family connection, would afford a fine days amusement, for such of the Springfield or Bloomington hunters who may happen to be in that neighborhood.

The prevailing error in hunting quail is, that as they very often get up under the feet or at most from four to six yards from the shooter, they are generally shot at when not more than 10 or 12 yards from the gun.

If they were allowed to reach from 25 to 30 yards away, many more would be killed; to say nothing about the better appearance on the table.

Should any young hunter, or even old one, be so nervous or impulsive that he cannot wait patiently as suggested, let him just try the experiment of cocking both barrels after the birds have risen.

When very young, I often walked between my father and his elder brother when partridge shooting.

My uncle always carried his gun at half-cock, and would steadily raise the hammers after the birds had risen. He would kill his double shot certain, a considerable time after his companion had fired both barrels.

Although my father was a good ordinary game shot, his brother could beat him 25 per cent. in the quantity of game killed in the day's shoot.

This was at a time when guns and ammunition were not so good as now, no choke-bores then.

I shall ever remember with pleasure some days snipe and chicken hunting with Capt. Bogardus, at Elkhart, Ill.; also at wild fowl with E. S. Cornell; quail and chickens with Jac. Karr; chickens with Charley Gordon, and wood-cock and quail in the timber with Henry Rowe; the last four near Gibson City, Ills.

They are all rare companions in the field, and at the top of the tree, as marksmen in each of the branches enumerated.

Talk of killing ducks and brant. Any infortunate creature that comes within 50 or 60 yards of Cornell, might save a lot of trouble by coming down at once, for if he just gets that gun of his to bear on them, it is all over.

There is still some splendid duck hunting in the Western States. The duck hunter's story, from the "Detroit Free Press," will give some idea of what it used to be.

"Speaking of duck shooting on St. Clair Flats," sighed an old citizen as he took a seat in a gun store yesterday, "I don't think there are as many birds up there as there was ten or fifteen years ago. Why, sir, the channels used to be just black with 'em, and they were so tame that you could knock 'em on the head."

Everybody sighed to think those good old days and ducks could never return, and the veteran hunter continued:

"I remember I was out one day in April. I got in among the bipeds, and how many do you suppose I counted?"

"Three hundred," ventured one of the audience after a long interval.

"Three hundred! Why, I always killed over a thousand every time I went out! No, sir, I counted over 16,000 great, big, fat, plump, delicious ducks, and then I had only counted those on one side of the boat!"

"How long did it take you?"

"I don't know, sir, I had no watch with me. Time is nothing to a man counting ducks. I counted aloud, and when the ducks were small I counted two for one. By and by I got tired of counting, and got ready for the slaughter."

"How many did you kill?"

"Well, now, I suppose I could lie about it and say I killed 900 or 1,000, but I'm getting too near the grave for that. No, I didn't kill a blasted one, and that's where the strange part of the story comes in. When I began to lift that gun up those ducks knew what I was up to just as well as a human being, and what did they do? Why, sir, about 200 of 'em made a sudden dive, swam under the boat, and all raised on her port-side at once and upset her! Yes, sir, they did, and there I was in the North Channel in ten feet of water, boat upset, night coming on, and I in my wet clothes."

"Well?"

"Well, I climbed up on the bottom of the boat, floated five miles and was picked up by two Indians. We towed that upset boat to an island, and here another curious thing comes in. Under the boat were 264 large, plump ducks. They had been caught there when she upset, and all we had to do was to haul 'em out and rap 'em on the head."

"Why, why didn't they dive down and get from under the boat?" asked an amateur duck-shooter.

"Why didn't they, sir—why didn't they? Well, sir, I might have asked 'em why they didn't, but it was late, a cold wind had sprung up, and I didn't feel like talking! All I know is that I counted over 16,000 ducks, was upset, captured 264, and have affidavits here in my wallet to prove everything I have stated. Does any man here want to see the documents?"

No man did. They all looked out of the windows and wondered if they could lie that way when they had passed three-score years.

I have heard of extraordinary scores being made in hunting wild fowl, but the largest bag really certified, was that of my friend Capt. E. E. Stubbs, with whom I lately shot a match at Little Rock, Arkansas, as recorded further on.

It was reported at the time in the "Semi-weekly Coast," and also in the "Gulf Weekly" newspapers. He was on a small tidal island, in a cove, about 3 miles from the main shore on the Mexican coast, and in 5 hours and 25 minutes, he killed 613 head of birds, each one shot at single and on the wing. There were 46 swans, 72 geese, 34 brant and 461 mallards and spoon bill ducks.

He used 627 cartridges of No. 4 shot, and it kept two Mexican ranchmen hard at work to gather in the game. They remarked "*Mellican man great shooter, big hunter,*" "*me hard work.*" "*He kill all de game.*" "*Dey jist comes right down when he pints dat way.*"

He also related to me that in 1875, when hunting alone, for the market, in Northwestern Iowa, during the months of September and October, he killed 1,957 prairie chickens, besides other game, using a brace of English pointers, one at a time, on alternate days.

I do not doubt either of the above statements, for I feel sure Capt. Stubbs would not relate anything untrue to me, and I can confidently say, that I consider him perhaps as good, if not the best shot I ever saw, both with the rifle and shot gun.

I think he can kill as many prairie chickens on the wing with a rifle, as any man I know (bar about 2 or 3) can do with a shot gun, and during this next summer I expect we shall see him trying his skill at pigeons 30 yards rise, English rules with his rifle, against crack men with the shot gun. Although I have had some very good shooting in America, I would rather not mention any of my best doings, as they are so completely put in the back ground by the above.

Much has been written and much jealousy and ill feeling expressed on the subject of the destruction of game in the Middle and Western States, by parties of hunters from the East, who ship all they kill either for market or to their eastern friends.

I have hunted every day during the season for three years, and can pretty well judge what quantity of game can be killed.

My opinion is that the scarcity and constant decrease in game is not caused by gunners, to a tenth part of what is supposed.

I was well equipped with guns, dogs, and the best hunting poney in the world. (Alas! since dead.) I could shoot double shots from the saddle as easily as from the ground, could turn her loose on the prairie for hours; on the slightest motion of raising the gun she would be firm as a rock, and in the tallest corn would thread her way with less damage than I could walk myself. I would mention, for the information of my friends in England, that the prairie chicken or pinnated grouse is much the same bird as the grouse of Great Britain.

The quantity of chickens and quails that I could kill, might have been raised easily upon two sections of land.

I maintain that the greatest enemies game has to contend with, are the farmer's dogs, hawks, snakes, mink, skunk, owls, crows, coons, opossums and foxes.

At almost every farm-house you will find two, three or four dogs, no matter what breed, so that they can *"kill a rat, and bite a tramp."* Some are called *full blooded* bird dogs, which are worse than any others when running loose, but they embrace every variety from the mastiff to the verriest cur poodle.

As a rule they are left to their own exertions for a living, and in the game breeding season accompany the teams when ploughing and cultivating the corn, so that nothing escapes them, breaking up the nests of the chickens and quail, scaring the old birds when sitting, and killing the helpless young by wholesale.

There are crows enough in Missouri and western Illinois to suck every egg laid; and crows also kill the young game. I have seen a gang of 1,000 at one time. No wonder game is scarce. Snakes also are very destructive to young game and eggs. I killed more than 100 rattle snakes in one summer and bull snakes out of number.

Again some of the farmers who do not hunt, take all the chicken's eggs for cooking purposes, so as to send their hen's eggs to market.

I was told by a farmer in Illinois last year, that he had used over 400 chicken's eggs in his house, all taken from 240 acres of land.

A regular hunter is the greatest friend to game, because he never omits an opportunity of killing vermin.

A chicken hawk requires a chicken or quail, at least, *every day in the year*; besides what they take extra when they have their young to provide for; so that a pair of those birds will kill more game in the year than a regular hunter, and I have always argued that by destroying on the average, a hawk or owl, besides other vermin every day I went out, that I was indirectly the means of preserving fifty head of game for every one I killed.

Farmers little think the benefit a sportsman is to them, in destroying the enemies of their domestic poultry.

Increased cultivation by utilizing sleughs and breaking up prairies must drive off prairie chickens, as it deprives them of insect feed, as well as places for seclusion and nesting.

Just a few lines here to chicken hunters: Study carefully the habits of your game, and save yourselves the time and trouble of beating over ground on which there is no chance of finding anything.

It is very pleasing to see dogs trained as for a field trial show, range over every yard of ground, quartering with almost mechanical exactness over perhaps a thousand acres of prairie after chickens, when not even 20 acres would be likely to hold a bird.

In Europe, where enclosures are small and game plentiful, and in some parts of this country where quails are abundant, such dogs are very beautiful to see; but a good chicken dog accustomed to hunting on the prairie, seems to know that the edges of the sleugh are most likely to hold game.

You will never find chickens in foul corn if there is any other within 3 or 4 miles, unless scared in early season by a hawk or from being shot into.

Chickens roost on open spaces in the prairie, so that vermin cannot easily reach them without detection, and there they will be found feeding at break of day, and again in the evening, on insects.

If in a country where small grain is cultivated, they will be in the wheat and oat stubbles, to feed early.

As the sun gets stronger in early season, they go to the edges of the slough on the prairies, where they can get the shade of the long grass, and watch for any indications of danger, and as a rule will stay there until about ten o'clock, when they leave for the shade of the corn, where they will remain, if undisturbed, until feeding time in the afternoon.

If the hunter is a stranger, and does not know the favorite corn fields, he can watch the flight of the birds from an elevated position, and after allowing them to rest for an hour, can go direct to where he will get good shooting.

Fresh broken land about the second or third year of cultivation is the most favorable resort; they dust and scratch in the shade, and can, in clean corn, watch every thing going on for some distance.

It is not unusual for birds to travel two or three miles to find the land they want; no wonder therefore that you may beat over a large tract of corn land full of weeds, without finding a single bird, even in a good chicken country.

Dogs that will keep close in, *and retrieve well*, are necessary in corn hunting; and if a space of about 20 or 30 yards is allowed between each gun in walking the rows, a good lot of ground may be beaten over during the hours of from 12 to 4 o'clock; after which the birds will be leaving for the stubble and pastures. Chickens rarely touch corn until insect and small grain feed is exhausted.

Chicken hunting, in corn which is often ten feet or more high, is very bad practice for finely broken young dogs; as hunting mostly out of view of their master, they are apt to take advantage of it, and break rules. I would rather at any time cleanly miss three shots, than leave a winged or wounded bird to suffer and become the prey of vermin. For that reason I have been this last two seasons allowing my dogs to go in at once for dead birds, because if you should tip the wing of a fully matured or old male bird, he will generally take the line of a row of corn, and go right away at his greatest speed until he reaches the long prairie grass, even if it is a quarter or half mile or more away.

If the dogs are made to drop to charge, and the bird gets 100 seconds start of the dog, unless he bleeds from his wounds, it can hardly be expected that a dog can trail a particular bird over perhaps twenty cross scents, and especially where it is stronger from the birds having been playing about for some time on the ground.

A bird running as fast as possible, leaves very little scent on dry ground in the summer season.

"Eyes open and mouth shut," is my motto in hunting. There is nothing will scare game so much as the human voice, and I maintain that one "*down charge*" spoken loudly and in anger, will set all the game on the alert within a quarter of a mile, and does infinitely more harm than a dog going direct to his dead game and returning quietly with it. Prairie chickens are not easily moved by a dog unless he should be a wild one, and many dogs will, in bringing dead game, especially quail, stand the live ones with the dead in its mouth.

I have many times, when on high ground, seen my dog Sancho coming in with a wounded bird, half to three quarters of a mile from the spot where it fell; it was only a question of time if he was not in at once, if it took him ten minutes, he was sure to get him before he returned. Dogs often get blame, for not finding what is thought to be a dead bird, when really there is no fault, as the game is perhaps some hundred yards away at the time he is sent for it; whereas, if the dog had been sent in at once, he would have recovered the bird before it had time to get round from the effect of the fall.

I cannot refrain from telling a little story. My friend Charley Gordon and myself were invited by some renters, on the 40,000 acre Sullivant farm, at Burroaks, in Ford Co., Illinois, to join a party in a prairie chicken hunt; as we were known pretty good shots, and had plenty of good dogs.

The whole neighborhood was called out. Every available gun, nearly a dozen, was looked up, and brought into requisition. Some had two barrels and only one hammer; others refused to remain at half or full cock, and had to be loosed from the thumb, and some had not been known to observe half cock for years, and of others, the barrels had some few apparently originally done service as gas pipes, about the time that article was introduced, and were secured to the stock by string or wire.

Every gun had a history and pedigree, of course, all *imported*, *genuine* articles; and most had killed ducks, geese, or chickens at 100 yards, and from 15 to 20 quails at one shot.

Soda water bottles suspended on strings, served for powder and shot flasks, and the palm of the hand for measures. Old newspapers answered instead of wads, and sometimes in a hurry a dram of powder would do for two ounces of shot. *"The more shot the better, but not much powder for fear of bursting the gun."*

Dogs of all sorts and sizes, rough and smooth, mostly called *full-blooded*, and descended from stock that could *"smell a chicken at a quarter of a mile." They had done it.* The whole party of men and dogs numbered nearly forty, so we spread out and went ahead. I preferred the right hand outside berth, as it appeared to me much the safest in that company; and stretching wide through the corn, we all went at it with a will.

One or two of the *"Nimrods"* led the hunt. They of course *knew* where the chickens were, *they* could find *"all you want"* in no time. "All you want" is a favorite expression in speaking of game, but what quantity it represents I never exactly found out. If it originated from *"We want but little here below,"* I certainly generally got it.

After toiling without my poney for about four hours in very foul corn, and moving only one bird, which I got outside in a road, and during which time I constantly told them *"we would never find any birds in such corn as that,"* we came to a well cultivated piece of about 100 acres.

As soon as I saw it, I said *"now boys look out for the chickens,"* and sure enough there they were.

For some hour and a half it was glorious fun! such volleys!! such shouting! such a row!! seven or eight shots at a single bird, and a very nice bundle of chickens was the result.

If Charley and I had been by ourselves, I really think we could have got 100. I visited that ground often afterwards and had fine sport.

I came across another well cultivated farm of 200 acres on the Sullivant estate. The occupier was a rare good hearted fellow named Furrey; he deserved a good crop. He said I was welcome to hunt his corn as often as I liked, he knew I would do him no damage, and for some time I had good sport there three days a week.

Good farming paid him well. It looked all of 80 bushels to the acre right through. He had two clever little twin sons, aged 12, who with another son about 18, and himself, entirely cultivated and managed 50 acres each, and they had reason to be proud of their success.

Some of the *small* freeholders detest hunters, as the *devil is said to hate holy-water*, and will if possible get some chance of swearing at you, and threatening vengeance. A renter, or a large owner seldom interferes, but the 40 acre man, *without the writings in his house*, takes every opportunity of asserting his authority, just to make believe that the place belongs to him, when, perhaps, having borrowed money at ten per cent. to get his land, he has not even a dollar of interest in it, and would be worse off than a renter if closed up. There are, however, many who will heartily welcome a stranger with a gun, and enjoy seeing a good shot; and more particularly clever dogs. But if you were to believe all you hear, there must be much more game in the country, than your dogs are able to find.

John Gillette, Esq., of Elkhart, Logan Co. Ills., a fine farmer of his own fine estate of nearly 10,000 acres, once said to me, "I have not the least objection to either Bogardus or yourself shooting over my land, whenever and wherever you like; because *you are hunters and you know your business*; and a regular hunter will do me no harm; but there are a lot of random young fellows come here and scare my cattle, and do me lots of injury, and I cannot allow them over my place."

A farmer in going his rounds, sees the same flock of quails, perhaps a dozen times in the course of the day, and supposes they are as many different lots, so that he tells you "*he can show you at least twenty gangs*" that is what they call them, "*gangs.*" I would have you beware how you get into a *gang* of quails near a farm house; for often you may get driven off at the point of a hay fork, by half a dozen men and dogs, if you get killing their "*pretty quails that come to feed with the fowls.*" I expect before two more Presidents are elected in this country, that in some parts game will be strictly preserved. At the present time the penalty for tresspassing in pursuit of game is much heavier than it is in England.

Once I marked a chicken down near to where a farmer's wife was picking corn; so I rode round the bird to get between it and the woman and beat away from her. I shot from the poney and killed the chicken, with my back toward the woman, but she told her husband that the shots hit her, and I was forbidden hunting on his ground afterwards, and often joked for having shot a woman. I had heard of guns shooting round stacks of corn, but that was the only instance of one throwing shot backwards, that I have had positive proof of.

Returning from hunting one day near Elkhart, Ills., I met a farmer, who asked me if I was fond of rabbitting. I replied *"just the sport I do like,"* he said, *"why don't you come to my place, you can get all you want, why you can just slay them!!!"* That settled it at once. I began to think. *Slay? Slay?* Ah! I remember now, why Samson *slew* a thousand Phillistines and *"all you want"* again! surely that means two sacks full at least. The snow was pretty deep, and next morning I started on my old poney with plenty of shells, three dogs and two new sacks; and after a long hunt I found the *shanty* in the timber.

My friend was just starting out for a log, so he said, *"put your poney in the stable and hunt round here anywhere, until I come back and join you."*

I found a bunch of seven quails and got two, and after a while I moved a rabbit which I killed. So after four hours work I gave it up in disgust, and just when I started for home he came back.

On describing my hunt to him, he explained. "*What! not found but one rabbit!!*" "*Why my dogs started two yesterday!!*"

I shall never forget that word *slay*. I could have *slayed* him if I dared.

C I could fill a large volume with pleasing reminiscences of dogs, &c., &c., for I had two pointers at the same time, Sancho, (see likeness of him on the cover) and Shot, that among other things were constantly standing on quail, when bringing in dead birds in their mouths, but I have no space at command, so must *hark back!*

In flushing game before a dog, it is best to walk up very quietly, or you may make him nervous and unsteady. Study carefully from the wind and circumstances, the probable position of the game, and do not walk *direct to it* or appear in a *hurry*, as most likely it is watching you, and will let you get much closer, if you appear to be going past it.

Try and drive your birds in the direction most easy to follow, and rise them against wind if possible, as they will not fly so swiftly.

If ducks, say a couple of mallards, are coming *right over you*, let them get well past before shooting; there is plenty of time for a double shot, and if you shoot under them from behind, they are more easily killed than from the front, as the feathers are softer.

I am convinced that one-half of the shots missed, thought to be out of range, would have been effective if the gun had been held more forward; as it must take longer for shot to travel 60 than 20 yards, and allowance has to be made for the time lost in *pulling trigger, fall of hammer, ignition of cap, combustion of powder and reaching the object*, which, however instantaneous it may all seem at first thought, would allow a bird in fast flight to travel several feet.

Often, when shooting at several birds, and one has dropped, you hear a companion say: "What a splendid shot," when, in reality, it was not the bird you aimed at but one several feet behind it that was killed; and if it had been a single bird fired at you would not have killed at all.

The great advantage claimed for the breech-loading gun is not only the rapidity of firing and reloading, but that however foul the barrels may be, the shells are each fresh and clean, and, moreover, the shot can be changed in a moment as occasion may require.

Sometimes when loaded for snipe with 10 shot, you suddenly come upon a chance of a shot at large game, your shells can be changed in a second, whereas you may as well have thrown a stone as shot at it with the charge of small shot.

In trap shooting, it is always advisable to have a supply of shells loaded with the Dittmar or smokeless yellow powder, for if shooting with the use of both barrels, now becoming so general, should the atmosphere be close and muggy, no matter what sort of black powder is used, if the bird goes straight away, the second barrel will be almost useless in 9 out of every 10 shots.

I had the pleasure of an introduction when in New York to Mr. J. Von Lengerke, the representative of the Dittmar Co. He presented me with 100 loaded shells for a trial, and they were used by the Englishman in the Bogardus-Rimell match at Pittsburgh, for the first barrel. He scored 90 dead in bounds and 9 over the fence, which was only 50 yards in front of the traps. Bogardus used Dittmar in his first barrel in same match and scored 96 in bounds and 3 dead over the fence, at 30 yards rise, five ground traps, under English rules.

The great secret in the use of Dittmar powder appears from the trials I have made, and which is also Mr. Lengerke's opinion, that the more perfectly the powder is confined in loading, the greater will be the power and of necessity the better will be the results.

I strongly advise the use of wads *without* any indentations, particularly for Dittmar powder, for in loading shells there is no necessity for them on the score of escape of air, as there was in the old muzzle loading times. If the indented wads are used, care should be taken that the air holes are not exactly over each other, but I think the makers of wads would do well to drop them altogether.

With a 10 bore, 9 lb. breech-loader, I use by measure $5\frac{1}{2}$ drams of C diamond grain Dittmar or Orange Lightning powder; a Baldwin dry wad to keep the grease from the powder; two thick, strong greased wads, *well rammed down* singly, and another Baldwin dry wad on the shot.

The brass shells I think far best for Dittmar powder, as they will admit of a wad a size larger than the paper shells, and the tighter the wad the better must the explosive power be confined in leaving the barrel. In loading with Dittmar it will be found a very great advantage to let the shell remain all night, or at any rate a few hours after the powder and the wads are well rammed down before putting in the shot, as it will admit of considerable more pressure on being struck with the mallet afterwards.

A rammer made of iron something in the same style as a wad-cutter, closely fitted to the shell, will keep the wads level and prevent the sides turning up.

Soft felt wads, or soft wads of any kind, are of *no use whatever* with Dittmar powder. I have cause to remember it, for I lost a good match through using them. My candid opinion is, that *properly loaded*, the Dittmar powder is as good, both for quickness and killing properties, as the best black powder ever made. That is my own experience.

Occasionally, perhaps, once in one or two hundred shots you may find a shell that appears defective, but that is also the case with all powders, because it is almost certain to arise from the raising of the wads, particularly in brass shells, or some error in loading.

Without wishing to favor any particular make of powder, I recommend every gunner to use the very best he can purchase; no cheap, dirty trash.

Orange Lightning is the make I always use in my matches. I do not say it is better than any other, but I have always found it alike, truly and thoroughly reliable, which is what I want.

I remember Bogardus used it when in England in 1875, and I believe has continued doing so up to the present time, and considers it *the best*.

We Britishers have a great notion of sticking to a good thing. and I purpose keeping to Orange Lightning as long as it maintains its present excellence.

A great difference of opinion exists on the merit of large and small bore guns, and large and small sized shot.

With a small bore gun, say No. 18, there would be double the friction that there would be from a 10 bore, because double the quantity of shot would be exposed to the inner surface of the barrel.

Friction means consequent loss of power and velocity, and loss of velocity means loss of penetration.

I am of opinion, without any actual scientific data to guide me. that there would be 25 per cent. greater velocity and power with a No. 10 guage gun, 5 drams of powder and 1¼ oz. of shot, than with an 18 bore gun loaded with 3 drams of powder and 1 oz. of shot.

All that may not be of much consequence in shooting at a *straight away* bird at 25 or 30 yards, but apply it to a fifty yards *quartering shot* and *it will astonish you*, and show the necessity of shooting well forward.

The larger the size of shot the greater the velocity; thus, No. 3 shot will travel 10 per cent. or more faster than No. 7, and consequently makes greater penetration, which will account for its killing at greater distance. (See addenda, page 31.)

After a common sense consideration of the subject, I have come to the conclusion that a 10 guage gun of 9 lbs. weight, 30 inch barrels, is the best suited for all purposes.

It is not too heavy to carry in the field, and is of sufficient weight to allow of 5 drams of powder and 1¼ oz. of shot, when handled by a person of ordinary physique.

If a gun is found to rebound seriously, it is obviated entirely, at a cost of 75 cents, by a rubber pad on the butt.

I use 5½ drams of best powder in matches, and can shoot 100 double shots without the least soreness of the shoulder or inconvenience to the nervous system from concussion, whereas without the pad, I should be almost unable to raise my arm at 100 double shots.

With regard to shot, I am much in favor of small sized shot as a general rule. No. 9 New York, with good load of powder behind, is very effective. Try it for the first barrel.

The original inventor of the double-barreled gun was either very stupid, or what is more probable, he was a left handed man, for certain it is that the triggers are placed in a favorable position for a left shouldered shot.

It would be found much handier in use if the first trigger was placed where the second now is, and the left barrel used first, as it is easier to move the finger forward than take it back, and it would glide more readily from one trigger to the other.

When I first noticed it, I changed them in my gun, and was delighted with the plan, but I foresaw that if it was adopted it would at first be very dangerous in the hands of strangers.

The first person to whom I showed it was a Welsh gamekeeper, almost always with a gun in his hand.

I explained it very carefully to him, and he liked it muchly, but was slightly offended as I cautioned him against accident when he began, as is usual to try the locks.

Almost on the instant off went the gun. He was, of course, handling the wrong hammer. Fortunately, I was clear of the muzzle, and no further damage was done than a few broken squares of glass in his employer's conservatory.

It is scarcely necessary to add that I replaced the triggers in their old form, and I leave it to a wiser generation to adopt the principle.

I cannot refrain here from noticing what appears to me a very *sad waste* of life, and food intended for man, in the wanton destruction of game, and particularly wild fowl, in the Western States, for the purposes of sport only, the birds when shot down being left to suffer and die a lingering death from starvation.

A great deal of this may be caused by the arbitrary laws passed in most of the Western States, prohibiting the exportation of game, even by residents.

I know instances in Iowa of hunters killing chickens wholesale and leaving them to rot upon the ground.

It is very one sided policy, for, as a rule, Eastern hunters will spend and leave more money in a neighborhood where they are hunting, than three or four times the value of the game killed, so that indirectly the landowners would benefit by encouraging hunters and it would be selling their game pretty dearly. A market hunter will carefully gather all he kills and send it for sale where anybody who has not the time or the opportunity to kill game for themselves, can buy it and enjoy a dish of game at a moderate cost.

A rich man, who has the means at disposal, to command the best hunting grounds, and with every facility to get large quantities of game, merely shoots it down for so-called sport and leaves the poor things to perish, oftentimes in a single day destroying and wasting what would be food for *fifty families*.

I would suggest to all such gentlemen who would not like to handle the proceeds of game sent to market, that they should send it free of cost to the nearest available hospitals, poor houses and public institutions, where the gift would be appreciated by the poor suffering inmates. The express companies would, doubtless, convey it free of cost. Another idea presents itself. Let the game be sent to market in the ordinary way and the proceeds given to some good charities, or handed over to the State Sportsmen's Association to provide a series of prizes at the annual tournament.

ADDENDA.

WHY LEFT QUARTERING SHOTS ARE GENERALLY KILLED.

If, instead of the sight being taken along exact line of barrels B to B, it should be done inadvertently from the left side of the rib C to C and dead on, if a left quartering bird, it will be equivalent to aiming at least two feet ahead at forty yards, and it will be a certain kill, if the motion of the gun is not stayed in pulling the trigger, for the bird will fly into the line of the charge and be struck well forward.

Should the shot be a right quartering one, and aim be taken in the same way from C to C, the effect will be exactly opposite and would be two feet behind the bird, which with a close shooting gun, would be a sure miss. [See diagram.]

On the contrary, if the aim be taken from the right side of rib, A to A, the right quartering shots would be killed and the left missed. Little need be cared for on that point, however, as it would very seldom occur that the gun was sufficiently on the chest to allow the sight to be so taken. It is well, therefore, as mentioned on page 8, to shoot well forward in right hand shots.

Remember, that if in the excitement of the moment the eye, although perfectly dead on the sight, should be, say the eighth of an inch, higher than the level of rib at breech, it would cause the bird to be overshot very considerably. On the other hand, if the eye should be below the level at back it would of necessity produce an undershot. The finest and most perfect aim at the muzzle is useless unless it is also correct at breech. All these things will account for so many misses, of which there seems no possible explanation at the time. Guns are seldom to blame for misses at any moderate distance—either the shooter himself or the loading doubtless being at fault.

On referring to page 59 it will be found that in the match between Bogardus and Rimell at Pittsburg, and in which 198 out of 200 birds were killed, with only 2 incomers, 10 out of 13 dead out of bounds were right hand shots hit undoubtedly a little behind, whereas every left hand bird was scored; and recently, in the Price-Oberg match for State Championship at Kansas City, Mo., right quartering birds only were missed. If experienced shots are liable to do this, it is very requisite for beginners to pay especial attention to keeping the gun perfectly upright in hand, and to take aim from the centre of rib at breech.

PREVENTION OF ACCIDENTS WITH GUNS.

Never carry a gun with the muzzle in a direction that it would be dangerous to life or property if accidentally discharged.

Remember that the muzzle is the only dangerous part of a gun. Keep it pointed, therefore, either to the sky or to the ground.

There is more to be dreaded from a companion's weapon than your own; do not allow him to hold his gun so that you can see down the barrels.

When going through or over a fence, put your gun at half or full cock, for if it should catch in anything, it will not explode as it would if the hammer rested on the cap and was slightly raised and loosed. Keep it well in front, muzzle upwards, with the hand in front of the trigger guard. If you should be in company the one following should bring his gun through the fence pointing backwards.

When expecting game, the gun should be carried on the left arm if your companion is on the right side; or in the left hand, with the muzzle sufficiently upwards to be safe.

The finger should never touch the trigger until the game is moved; for if a stumble or fall occur in walking, and the finger is inside the guard, it is almost certain to cause an explosion.

The hammers should *never* be resting upon the cap or striker, *it is very dangerous*, as a very slight blow or concussion from a fall would cause a discharge. For 25 or 30 years I have carried my gun at full cock without an accident, and if the locks are good, I have always considered it the safest way.

If snow or mud gets into the barrels be careful to clear it well out before shooting. Many good barrels are either burst or bulged from some substance, even a wad being left in the muzzle.

When getting into, or out of a wagon, do not pull your gun after you. Keep it in front with the point well up.

A breech-loading gun need scarcely ever be loaded except when expecting game; but a few shells should be kept in the most convenient place in case of hurry.

Never take a loaded gun into a house, but either draw the shells or take off the caps.

"This to your memory keep."

Under no circumstances whatever attempt to de-cap or re-cap a loaded shell, but carefully draw the charge first. If a metal shell, keep it well in front, so that the charge would be clear of you in case of explosion; and if a paper shell, better lose the shell by cutting it through to save the ammunition, than run the risk of taking off the primer.

In loading shells keep them well away in front, and be careful that the primer does not rest upon any hard substance, but have holes drilled out in the centre of the stand.

Have metal shells properly fitted for the chamber of your gun, and do not lend them, for if used in a gun of slightly larger calibre than your own, they will burst or bulge, and be useless for your own afterwards.

When loading a gun place the butt upon the foot and incline the muzzle *well outwards* quite *clear* of your head. If one barrel is fully loaded it should be turned farthest away, keeping the hand clear of it, and only the smallest portion of the finger that is necessary should be over the loaded barrel in using the ramrod. Both barrels should be at half cock, as the escape of the gas allows the powder to be driven well into the tube.

Take care not to leave tow or rag in the breech when wiping out the gun; it may be fired by the first discharge and igniting the powder in reloading, may cause a fatal accident by exploding the contents of the powder flask,

Have the caps properly fitted to the tube, so as not to burst in putting on; they will be easily taken off, and not liable to be lost.

A spare tube and wrench, a shell extractor, knife, screw-driver, piece of cord or string, and some small money will be found useful to a hunter.

Never put away a gun without wiping and oiling outside, and examine the locks often for fear of water and rust.

Wash the barrels of a muzzle loader very often, for in damp weather a large portion of the powder will be wetted, and becomes caked when forced down into the breech.

Be careful that your shells are properly loaded, and carry at least two sizes of shot for ordinary use. A few with buck and B B shot should be kept very conveniently for large game, or long shots at flocks of geese or ducks. I have killed 8 and 10 ducks at a double shot into a large lot at 100 yards, with 6 drams of powder and $\frac{3}{4}$ oz. of B B shot.

Great caution should be taken if the wad over shot should become loose, to remove it before putting in another cartridge; for if the weight of shot should force the wad to the muzzle of the gun, it would be almost certain to burst or bulge the barrel at the next discharge.

Many fine guns are spoiled by this simple thing, and either the maker of the gun or the powder (particularly if Dittmar or any other new explosive should be used), gets blamed for a casualty over which they have no control, and the real cause is never known.

It is not very likely that the strength of any powder (even if 20 drams were used), would be powerful enough to damage a barrel which has been tested to stand many times that power before leaving the factory.

In resting a gun upon the ground *never* place the hand over the muzzle; it is *very dangerous*.

Not long since I was hunting with a young man who was very careless with his gun. Several times I had occasion during the day to caution him, as he would place the butt end on the ground with the hammers on the caps, and his hand over the top of the barrels.

He seemed to regard my advice very lightly, forgetting the adage that "The *young* men *think* the old men are fools, but the *old* ones *know* the young men are."

About two weeks afterwards he was in a wagon with a spring seat, holding his gun in the same manner, and in going over some rough ground the jolting caused the spring seat to raise the hammer sufficiently to discharge the gun and carry away the whole of the centre of the hand and cripple him for life.

If his gun had been at half or full cock, it would not have occurred.

Even the breech loader is not altogether free from liability to accident.

A few weeks since I handed my gun for five minutes to a youth to hold, while I was away to get a drink of water.. I took precaution to draw the shells, but the young hopeful amused himself by cocking and hitting the hammers upon the strikers, and as there were no shells the force drove the pins further than usual, and the spiral spring failed to throw one of them back again into its place.

On replacing the shells I did not observe the projecting pin, and on closing the gun it pressed upon the primer, causing the cartridge to explode, and I had to thank God that the muzzle was pointed in a proper direction, which most likely saved the life of one of the party of men and dogs.

Since writing the above, I attended a small shooting match in the country, to which I was invited to act as referee, and although perhaps not more than 50 or 60 persons present, I met with four that had been the victims of gun accidents, admittedly through sheer negligence.

The first had his hand shockingly mutilated from a shell bursting when he was de-capping it. He had lost the thumb and two fingers entirely. The second had a hole drilled out through the center of the palm of the hand from the gun exploding in a somewhat similar way to the accident described in a foregoing page—hand over muzzle, but this case resulted more distressingly than even the other, for it left him with paralysis of the entire arm, so that he will never be able to raise his hand to his mouth again.

The third was totally blinded in one eye from the gun of a companion being discharged in his direction while duck hunting. The fourth was a case of holding the fingers over a loaded barrel while filling the other. The lock was worn, and the concussion or shake in ramming a hard wad in a foul gun caused an explosion and carried away nearly the whole of thumb and two fingers.

There may even have been others among the company present who could have related piteous and woeful tales of misery resulting from foolish and incautious use of firearms, but it did not occur to me to inquire for them.

ADDENDA.

In the earlier editions I omitted to warn my readers against the use of mixed shot. My attention has been directed to it from having received several letters asking my opinion on that subject.

If you use a mixture of sizes it is obvious that as the heavy shot travels faster than the light the larger shots, if behind, will either bump against the smaller from increased velocity, destroying the force of both and causing them to fall to the ground before reaching the object; or, if it should not strike directly behind, will cause the smaller shot to scatter in all directions and interfere with others out of line. It is advisable therefore to use shot that is not only regular in size and shape, but in weight. I am of opinion that to the irregularity of shot more than to anything else is to be attributed the great difference of pattern and count with the same gun at different times—and to the fact that sometimes 20 or 25 per cent. of the shot by actual count are lost altogether from collision and consequent dropping—where the shot is irregular in size.

REMARKS ON PIGEON SHOOTING.

Pigeon shooting from the trap is now becoming a great institution in this country, and from the immense gatherings of splendid shots that I have seen, it would become exceedingly popular I think if the system of increased distances at handicaps and five ground traps was generally introduced.

The principal argument I find advanced against the ground trap is that the birds here will not rise well from them, forgetting that it is natural for a bird to try for liberty.

There is, indeed, good reason why they do not fly when the trap is loosed, for the poor birds are too often physically incapable from bad treatment and neglect.

If they were as expensive here as in England they would be better looked after. Coming from a journey, birds should have a day or two of rest in a good barn, with a plentiful supply of water and sand; should have double the present room given them in traveling, the coops being high enough to stand up in and move freely.

Pigeons should be kept in a large, well ventilated barn, with small, round perches not more than $\frac{1}{2}$ to $\frac{3}{4}$ inch in thickness, and not allowed to be seen or approached by any one except the usual feeder.

Three or four times every day tame birds should be well scared by being driven in the barn with either a noisy whip or a switch that will hit without hurting them, and lead them to expect a whipping every time they see a person, but wild birds should be kept as quiet as possible.

Wicker baskets or hampers are best when on the shooting ground to protect them from the sun and allow free ventilation, without exposing them to the view of spectators.

The wildest looking birds, and those of cleanly and healthy appearance should be selected for present use.

Birds should be fed regularly and very moderately, morning and evening, with a mixture of all sorts of grain and seeds available, and supplied at all times, with some such as the following mixture:

A peck of old building mortar.
A peck of crushed bricks.
A peck of good fresh sand or small gravel.
One and a half pounds of Cumin seed.
Quarter pound of bay salt, well mixed and a little given fresh every day.

Water should be provided at least once per day in clean vessels so made, that being shallow in some parts, the birds can bathe freely.

In selecting for the trap, every squab and sickly, weak bird should be rejected and put into a separate room, which should serve as a hospital, as it is far better to keep such birds at home for a short time until they can fly, than to irritate and annoy the shooter with such trash, for they are equally unsatisfactory whether with plunge or ground traps.

Feed is cheap enough in this country that to keep them a few days would not be so serious an expense, and would be compensated for by not having any of them refused as being non-flyers.

I think it would be a very excellent plan to clip the tails of wild birds at the time of catching them, and before being cooped at all. It would prevent their getting filth and dirt upon the feathers and I am quite certain that the birds leave the traps much better and more regular with the tails a little shortened, and more particularly so with the long, swallow-tailed male birds.

Wild birds will be sure to fly well from traps, if not exhausted from traveling and want of food and water.

Many tame birds, either from being young or from having been home bred and constantly near to human beings, will not care to fly either from ground or plunge traps; for if thrown from the latter they generally turn to the ground in a moment, and more particularly so if *dead birds* are allowed ungathered near the traps.

Tame birds will almost sure fly to the nearest building; it is advisable to place the traps so that in getting towards it the bird will be going straight away.

After keeping some 250 wild birds for two weeks perfectly quiet, I found they went from traps much faster when fed only once per day; for if allowed unlimited food a pigeon will become fat and lazy in a few days, for want of exercise.

I would, however, recommend that the barn where wild birds are kept should have a stretched canvass under the roof to prevent their being injured from flying upwards when scared, and striking the head against the top of the room.

In the Bogardus-Rimell, Lucas-Price, and Bogardus-Jewett matches at wild birds, out of 1,200 trapped, only 13 turned towards the shooters and were killed inside the circle of the traps. The new ground traps, where the bird is put in at the back and cannot turn, were used on those occasions. *See advertisement.*

The wild pigeon acts as nearly as possible like the English starling, and is very little larger than the common dove of England. He is off like a shot when the trap opens, and is, therefore, exactly suited for ground traps.

My opinion has often been asked as to the difference between the wild bird of this country and the English blue rock; so called because originally they were bred in the holes in the rocks or quarries, on the northeast coast of England.

The principal of the best birds now obtained for the London Gun Clubs, are from the large farmers in Lincolnshire, where houses are very thinly scattered. The high price paid for them for heavy matches, induces them to breed only from the small blue bird, although some of the white ones are equally fast and good, and calculated to flurry a shooter if one is occasionally introduced.

The rock is unquestionably stronger than the wild bird, but is considerably larger, and after seeing some good wild birds trapped in the Bogardus-Rimell matches at New York and Pittsburg, and recently in the Lucas-Price matches at St. Louis, I am decidedly of opinion that if the wild birds are in really good condition, they are quite as difficult to make a score with as the best English rock. It is useless to disguise the fact, however, that birds are seldom trapped here in good order; they frequently are sent by express five or six hundred miles, and suffer badly from fright and privation, and are seldom taken from the coops in which they travel until trapped.

Birds should be fed and well watered as near to the time of shooting as convenient, and have water at the coops, if possible, in very hot weather, and not be exposed to sun or rain.

The tails should be cropped about an inch to keep them free from wet and dirt in traveling, and if not required for shooting that day, they should be loosed in the barn before sundown to allow for feeding time.

A little well soaked corn is a good substitute, if it is not convenient to water them in the coops.

With a plunge trap not one bird in three ever makes an effort to fly. They are jerked, or rather plunged into the air, just as a *dead cat* might be; and are shot at when they have reached the highest point, or as they are dropping, and before they have had time to extend the wings.

There is not a shadow of a pretext for saying that such *child's play* is any criterion of ability in the field; as it is not known there the exact spot from which the bird will rise, and there birds do not fly downwards as is nearly always the case from the plunge trap.

Just one little bit of advice to promoters of shooting tournaments in this country:

While I am quite willing to give every credit for the great trouble and expense bestowed upon the general arrangements for the comfort and pleasure of the visitors, they seem altogether to overlook the principal thing, and that is the condition of the birds to be used. It is very like the play of Hamlet with the principal character omitted.

An extra outlay of $50 for a good barn would not be too much to be expected, when, as I have been told, it is not an unusual thing for a profit of from $500 to $1,000 to be made on a tournament, besides the advantage to the town where it is held.

In Europe, the party furnishing the birds also traps and handles them, and every bird hanging when the trap is pulled over, is refused *and not paid for*. That is the proper system to get birds that can fly. So long as plunge traps are tolerated, one bird is as good as another if it is not actually dead when carried to the trap. I saw at a shoot a few days since the boys took the birds to the traps by the wings.

I was referee lately at a plunge trap match, where on a bird being challenged for shot marks and picked, the shoulder was found to be broken. There was no trace of shot marks, but some blood issued from a feather hole in plucking, the color of which and of the wound satisfied me that the injury had been caused quite 24 hours before. No question could have arisen with the ground trap because the bird could not have left the ground.

The five trap handicap system causes a little more trouble for the scorers and managers, and requires a little time to get appreciated, but when once thoroughly understood it will be enjoyed. It has entirely superseded the H. & T. one trap, one barrel plan in Europe, and nothing else is now known there. The plunge traps have never been seen there but they would not be tolerated, as they shoot for money and bet largely, therefore, a bird must fly or be refused.

Club competition in teams is thoroughly an American institution and a most enjoyable and sociable style of contesting among gunners, worthy of every encouragement if conducted upon more just and equitable terms than I have observed.

I would not have each team shoot off all their birds *in a squad* as at present, because much favoritism can be shown. One team may shoot when the weather, birds, wind, light and every other circumstance may be in their favor, and another may shoot when the sun is in their eyes, or when exhausted, and when the elements, birds and everything else is against them.

Let the whole company of contestants shoot separate and distinct as in an ordinary sweepstakes, and instead of following each other at the score *as a team*, let the position of every shooter be put on the list by drawing for places, and each round shot through in regular order. By that means the man who supplies the birds and the trappers could show no favor.

The spirit of the competition would be kept up until the end of the shoot. The scores of each team could be taken out and added together for the result.

Instead of 10,000 or 12,000 birds being required for a week's tournament, as it is with plunge traps, and squad shooting in classes, adopt the English system of five traps, each bird being gathered, and the trap refilled each shot; birds well prepared to fly from ground traps and not thrown into the air and shot at when the movement of the bird represents more nearly the gyrations one might expect if a lobster was used instead of a bird, and I feel perfectly satisfied that 99 out of 100 *genuine sportsmen* would go home better pleased in having seen 50 hundred good *shots on the wing* than the slaughter of some ten thousand half dead, ill-fed birds, tossed into the air and shot without exhibiting the slightest motion of a bird in flight.

Where will be found the genuine lover of field sports who would not rather kill say 12 brace of prairie chickens or quails, or even 20 couples of jack snipe, over a brace of good dogs, than bag four or five times that quantity of game if driven to the muzzle of his gun?

So with trap shooting. Give up the idea that sport and enjoyment consists in the slaughter of the largest given quantity of birds, and encourage the practice of less in number, and the exhibition of that sort of skill, the excellence of which will qualify for the enjoyment of that most exhilerating sport to be found on the prairies and in the stubbles.

A shooting ground ought, on the score of economy, to have a good, well-ventilated pigeon house, so that if birds are left over they need not be wasted and kept in coops huddled together before being required for a shoot. It is far better to have birds on hand several days before a tournament than run the risk of delay or neglect of expressage and consequent annoyance, to say nothing of the better condition of the birds.

There should be a compartment for tame birds, another with canvass lining over head for wild ones, and one for a hospital which should have a few perches close to the floor, say about 4 to 6 inches, as sickly birds are often illtreated by the strong ones, and wild and tame birds do not get on well together.

A barn can be easily put together so that the birds can neither see nor be seen. Get lumber 8 feet long and set them upright to overlap each other, one board in front of two, about $1\frac{1}{2}$ in. with about same distance between outer and inner boards, and make the roof in same way. By that means you get perfect ventilation and perfect isolation.

On the ground of humanity, every bird should be gathered after each shot, and killed at once. In the Lucas-Price matches, at St. Louis, I first introduced dogs to bring in the birds, as it saves much time. Lucas' setter Don and my pointer Sancho did the work alternately, and nearly every bird was brought in by the time the next one was trapped, and a dog shows no favor, but goes straight to the bird regardless of the stake depending upon its being scored.

I attended a large club shoot where six or eight boys were employed to fill six traps at express speed. The birds were thrown into the air by the plunge trap, and after killing them as fast as possible all the day, they felt pleasure, I suppose, in being able to relate to their friends *who knew nothing about the merits* how many birds they had killed in a given quantity, and that is called sport.

One of the rules of the club was that the bird should be shot at *when on the wing*, and that the gun should be *below the elbow until the bird was on the wing*. If those rules had been strictly observed, not one in 10 was rightly scored, for they were shot at long before their wings had ever been extended in proper flight, such as a bird would take in the field.

Many birds, especially wild ones, get just the tip of the wing broken when caught or in traveling or handling, which can be easily observed in ground trap shooting, as, being unable to rise, they are rejected, but if thrown from a plunge trap, even if never touched with a single shot, they are allowed as a dead bird, and it is not at all unlikely where it is known what shooter the bird is intended for when trapped, the wing may have been broken intentionally.

In shooting from five traps with a dice, the trapper never can tell who will have the bird, therefore no collusion or favoritism will avail.

I was once explaining to the secretary of a large club how much better it was to shoot from the ground trap, and he told me that the five trap plan was *too slow* for their club, as the trap had to be filled each shot, and they could not kill enough birds.

Of course, the ground trap shooting does not give the man who supplies the birds so much profit as the plunge trap does, but I hardly suppose the pigeon purveyor is to be considered to the detriment of the whole body of shooters.

Class shooting not being known except in America, it is perhaps well just to explain it. Every man in the shoot proper at 21 yards has a certain number of birds. All that make a clean score go into the first class, and are entitled to shoot off for the first prize at 26 yards. Those that miss one bird shoot off for second prize at 26 yards, and those missing two, shoot for third prize at 26 yards. If there are any ties in the second contest, all go back next time to 31 yards and remain at that distance until shot through, so that the prizes do not go to the best shots. It is a delusion and a snare to induce a novice to believe that he has a chance of winning.

The system is open to many very serious objections. A man who can not kill more than 8 birds out of 10 at 21 yards rise from the plunge trap, has no right to expect a prize for *good* shooting, which should be the object in all competitions.

It is not usual in other sports. In horse racing, only the best get prizes; whereas, here the second best gets nothing. It is also open to collusion, for you will often find that 3 or 4 of the very best shots "*form a pool,*" and instead of honestly contesting for the first prize, they agree before starting to divide winnings, and then some *intentionally* miss one, two or three birds, as the case may require, by carefully watching the score book.

The ordinary shooter or novice who has scored his eight birds, finds himself in the ties at an increased distance, competing with men who would on their merits be in the first class; therefore, unless some accident occurs, this *clique or ring of sportsmen* pocket nearly, if not all the prizes, and quietly divide them equally afterwards.

This little game is played nearly everywhere; not only by so-called *professional* shots, but as much by those whose *position* and *pretensions* should place them above suspicion. A man may argue that he has a *right* to miss one or more birds if he likes; but I maintain that he has *no such liberty* according to all notions of *propriety*. So soon as he enters the arena of public competition, he becomes, so to speak, a public man; and his acts are open to public criticism. The spirit and meaning of all competition is, that *every one should do his best*, and the shooter who kills his eight out of 10 birds, becomes properly and justly entitled to contest for the third prize. But if another man intentionally misses two birds and gets into the third class, he commits a *wilful and deliberate fraud* upon every man who has to meet him in the ties for that prize.

I do not find fault with class shooting if *honestly* carried out; the shoot proper being merely a trial from which to obtain a handicap of three classes; but after having found the exact handicap of each shooter, the three prizes ought to be of *equal value* to make it fair and just; after all *that* is done you cannot tell whether every one *has* shot honestly and square in the trial; that is the weak point, and there is no remedy for it.

An owner of race horses may say that he has a right to lose a race if he thinks proper, but in England the Jockey Club steps in and says "*your horse is public property so soon as he comes under our rules,*" and then let him lose a race intentionally and be detected, he would never have a chance to run another horse, nor would the jockey be allowed to ride one.

I say, therefore, that it is far better to do away with such conditions altogether, if they encourage *roguery and deceit*, and shoot under rules that can offer no inducement for anything but straightforward, honest competition. No other country in the world can produce such a lot of fine shots as there are here; it puzzles me, therefore, how such an enlightened body of sportsmen should have tolerated class shooting for such a length of time. Let the prizes be given to the three or more best shots, to be shot out bird for bird after the ties, if any, and save time and expense of pigeons. Under the present system, too much is expended on the birds in shooting off ties, leaving very little for the winners in ordinary sweeps.

In order to give a reasonable chance to an inferior shot, let all be handicapped according to ability, at from 24 to 30 yards rise;

and if the man at 24 yards is not a match for the very best at 30 yards, he cannot be said to have sufficient ability to expect reward in any competition.

There cannot be a greater fallacy than for an inferior shot to suppose himself on equal terms with a champion, because there are several classes; as many prizes as are given, so many first class men will go for them, and it is unfair then for him to subscribe an equal amount to the pool.

With a moderate entry of, say 50, at any State tournament, it is 1,000 to 1 against a novice getting a prize, unless he happens to have a score to himself unnoticed, and not have to shoot off the ties.

If a novice wanted a match single handed for money, the first class man would lay him $500 to $50, knowing it is 500 to 1 against his winning at equal distances; and that nothing short of some accident could prevent the giver of odds from taking it. But if properly handicapped, every man can stand a fair and equal chance of getting a prize, as the *best* can only make a given score at five trap shooting at 30 yards, if good birds.

In horse racing it is well known that weight will bring a pony and a race horse on equal terms; so in handicap pigeon shooting. Every man who can use a gun at all, should have a *good, fair* and *square* look in, which he can get in a handicap, and not throw his entrance money into a vortex. At present he stands in much the same position to a first class shot as a jackal does to the lion, simply provides him with food.

I know of an instance where, at one of the State Tournaments of 1879, a fine shot, who actually made the best score of the entire week, did not get a prize of a single cent, just because he was *not in a ring*, and it so fell out, that he, like Haidee in Don Juan—
"Forgot,
Just at the very moment she should not."

We wish to see every good, honest sportsman, handle some of the chips occasionally, and not find himself $75 or $100 out of pocket every time he favors a tournament with his presence.

Again, to bar a man from shooting because we think him a little better than ourselves, is very poor encouragement for excellence, and is *mean* and *cowardly* in the extreme; it offers every inducement for a shooter to lose intentionally sometimes, so that no one should know how good he really is.

In ordinary general shoots a champion should be put so that he may have a chance to win, and *then* there should also be prizes offered sometimes *for all on equal terms* to give some encouragement for ability.

I could relate two instances at least, where a stranger was actually barred, or as it was facetiously termed, *ruled out*, from an open competition for no other reason than that they did *not* know him; but he was unfortunately in the company of a good shot, and it was supposed they thought good shooting was as infectious as small pox.

Ask the "*champion wing shot of the world*" if he was ever *barred*, or *ruled out* of an open sweepstakes in any of his European excursions. I expect that he will tell you that not only was he invited to join in everything on *the same terms* as their *best* shots, but that when he won he was heartily congratulated on his success.

In trap shooting, holding the gun *below elbow* until the bird is on the wing, is an unnatural and uneasy position; and I will venture my reputation that no one ever carries his gun *so* when walking up to his dogs on game.

If you wish to make killing more difficult, it might be carried so far as to load the gun after the bird has been loosed. I have seen men in a position at the trap, that arms, legs and gun, forcibly reminds one of the collapsed sails of a windmill after a tornado. *See sketch on cover.*

Let the shooter hold his gun under the shoulder in as easy a position as he would in the field, and keep it there until he says "Pull." *See sketch on cover.*

It is impossible for the referee, wherever he may be placed, to see the gun and the bird at the same instant. It often gives rise to dissatisfaction, and leaves the shooter too much at his mercy.

The very moment the shooter says "pull," the referee can turn to see that the bird is well on the wing when shot at, under the English rules.

It is nothing unusual to see scores of 45 to 48 out of 50 killed, at 21 yards, plunge traps, with sickly birds, of which perhaps a third or more never could have got over the boundary line anyhow, if never shot at; but let the birds be good, and well cared for, rise 30 yards from five ground traps, 5 yards apart, and the wind behind the birds, and open 80 yards boundary; and the man who kills more than 40 out of his 50, can at once throw down the gauntlet for championship.

There can be no pleasure in making the killing of pigeons in a competition so great a certainty. With the five trap shooting it is more difficult, and tests the skill of the performer to a much greater extent.

Granted, it is perhaps gratifying to see your name in the "*Chicago Field*," or some local paper, with a lot of straight strokes instead of duck's eggs, but if all meet on fair terms, merit will come to the front.

In this great country where "Liberty" is on every coin, and "Equality," "Fraternity" and "Freedom" is on everyone's tongue, all men, so long as they conduct themselves honestly, and uprightly, should be welcomed in trials of skill and excellence.

"Is he a gentleman, or blackguard? Which?
A gentleman!! He acts as sich!!"

ADDENDA.

Nothing could better illustrate the utterly utter absurdity of class shooting than the following in "FOREST AND STREAM" answers to correspondents, Dec. 8, 1881. It speaks for itself. The very idea of a man getting a prize for missing every shot!!!

"GLASS BALLS.—Please answer the following: A, B, C, D and E engaged in a sweepstake match at 5 balls each, 3 prizes, class shooting. A breaks 5, B, C and D breaks 4 each and E misses them all. Who is entitled to 3d prize? Ans. E."

No doubt the answer is correct, for it is quite in keeping with the whole system of class shooting!!

HANDICAPPING.

Every State Association should, before the commencement of the shooting season, fix the handicap distance of each member for the year, which will continue, subject to any penalties for winning under rule 26 of the shooting code.

The basis for adjusting the distances should be taken as under from 24 to 30 yards.

24 yards, a known uncertain trap shot.
25 yards, a novice at pigeon shooting.
26 yards, a good game shot without experience at the trap.
27 yards, a known good trap shot.
28 yards, a fine trap shot and private winner.
29 yards, a large public winner.
30 yards, a champion shot on the wing.

Each member should be furnished with a certificate of membership of his State Association or Club, on which should be stated his handicap shooting distance, so that if he was taking part in any tournament outside his own State, the production of this certificate would entitle him to shoot at his settled distance, otherwise not being known he may expect to be handicapped at the extreme distance. The penalties for winning for each day will be found in rule 22, and in a tournament the winner of each large stake might fairly be penalized say 2 or 3 yards during the week, so as to give others a chance.

I am afraid we are too apt to call any man a professional who is a little better shot than ourselves and likely to take from us the paltry dollars subscribed to the pool.

Ask a shooter what is a professional shot? He will most likely reply, giving the name of some one entered against him of whom he has a wholesome dread, *as being one*, and would join in a crusade to *rule him out* right away on the least intimation that he would be backed if he proposed it.

It reminds me of an answer I saw once as to the difference between orthodoxy and heterodoxy. Orthodoxy is my doxy, and heterodoxy is any body else's doxy.

Some time since, I attended a shoot at Wenona, Ills., at considerable expense, and was *ruled out* of an open sweepstakes, on the ground *that if I was not then a professional I would be next week*, as I was advertised to shoot Bogardus for the championship of the world in a few days afterwards. At Indianapolis I was asked to withdraw from a sweepstakes on the promise that I should *certainly shoot in the next*, but although there were some twelve or fifteen shot in the first, not a single man would enter against me for the second.

Referring to professional shots: I should very much like to know what a professional shot is that, he should be *barred* or *ruled* out of an open shot in this free country?

If it is that to get a living at trap shooting constitutes a professional shot, I have never yet met with one that could succeed in the business in England. A few that have tried it might, perhaps, be found in the county poor houses.

Whether a man kills game and sends it to market or gives it away, it makes very little difference; there are many who are constantly hunting, who are not thought professionals or market hunters, who are, from constant practice, enabled to take most of the club prizes from others who, perhaps, handle a gun about once a month.

This difference of skill and ability cannot be remedied by class shooting, but handicapping will give each a fair chance.

There are lots of instances where men shoot matches for money, and do not hesitate to share the proceeds of the gate, and yet maintain their positions in high toned clubs. If a shooter of lower grade does the same thing, he is dubbed a professional at once.

I knew I would not be called a professional shot in my own country, so I thought I could get some exact information by asking the question from the "Chicago Field," and I got the following verys traight and highly sensible reply.

TRAP SHOOTING.

"W. G. P.—Let me know in your next what constitutes the difference between a "professional pigeon shot" and an "amateur pigeon shot." Ans.—A professional trap shot is one who makes his living mainly or entirely by trap shooting. An amateur is one who shoots occasionally for his own sport. An amateur loses his title to be called an amateur as soon as he engages in any contest for added money, purse, prize or gate money in which a professional is engaged. But the line of demarcation is not drawn in this country in this sport as it is in other sports, for if it were so drawn and enforced, there would be few of our crack shots that could lay just claim to be called amateurs."

After that I need not say anything, except that the sooner the term is dropped the better, for there is scarcely a good shot in the country that has not at some time or other been directly or indirectly tainted with the professional disease.

As well might a lot of lawyers or doctors endeavor to prevent another who, from extra study and assiduity, or a little more knowledge, has acquired a local reputation and is enabled thereby to command larger fees and increased business, *from practising against them*, as for a man to be prevented shooting for prizes because he has attained a little more skill than others. One of these days we shall hear of an amateur runner being objected to, and on being questioned: "Did you not run against 'Time' a few weeks ago?" I did. "Did not 'so and so' the professional run also against 'Time' for money?" He did. Then, as you contended against "Time," and "Time" had previously contended against a professional for money, you must, of course, be one. You are *ruled out*, sir." Not at all worse than I was served at Wenona.

Since writing the above, I came across a singular case in the "Chicago Field" of yesterday, Sept. 18th:

Not long since I noticed in an account of a large State shoot, I am inclined to think it was in Iowa, but cannot be sure, that a well known sportsman who, by some good fortune, took the first money on the first day's shooting, was *barred* at a meeting of the Association that same evening as being a professional shot.

I have not the pleasure of being intimate with him, but I thought at the time it was a very unsportsmanlike proceeding, for, having noticed his scores at different shoots since I have been in this country, I imagine that he has been as much the *jackal* and spent as much money freely in pigeon shooting as any man in his State.

Now, I notice with pleasure that this sportsman upon whom the injustice was practiced, is announced in conjunction with four *real honorables* and one *real captain* as a judge at a large State Association field trials, to commence this month. One of the gentlemen connected with the "Chicago Field" was *complimented* with the offer of a similar appointment, but was reluctantly obliged to decline the *honor* in consequence of his position on that journal.

Since the above remarks upon " professional shots " were written, I notice in the *Chicago Field* a challenge, which I cannot refrain from making some allusion to; and as it is an open offer, I presume I am at liberty to refer to it.

" A CHALLENGE.—The St. Louis Gun Club have authorized us to make the following challenge: The club will shoot ten men against the same number of men, who have been members of any regularly organized club six months' previous to the date of this challenge (professionals and market-shooters barred) for one thousand dollars a side; thirty wild birds each man, ten at 21 yards, ten at 26 yards, and ten at 31 yards rise, plunge traps. The match to be shot in St. Louis, and twenty dollars allowed each man for traveling expenses. Gate money to be divided, and the winning side to pay for the birds."

If ever a challenge was issued more strongly flavored with the *professional* element, I never saw it. 20 gentlemen, members of high-toned Gun Clubs, dividing *gate money*! Again, twenty dollars to be allowed each *gentleman* for traveling expenses. Now if such challenge had stipulated that the match was to be shot for the "*proud title of supremacy,*" choice of place to be decided by tossing, free admission to the public, and each man to pay his own expenses, cost of birds, and a good dinner and wine afterwards, I could appreciate it.

The conditions here are such that the verriest exhibition shooter, whose sole existence depended upon his gun, could not have been made to appear more like a money-making transaction than this one does.

Again, what has the poor *market hunter* done, that he is to be lowered in the *scale of creation*, and not thought fit to consort with your *club man?* Is this a Republican doctrine? I cannot detect what difference it makes to a farmer whether your *high-toned hunter* or your *market hunter*, kills his game and takes it off his land. I should not be at all surprised if your market-hunter does not leave more game behind him at the farm houses than the others, at least it is what I have learned from my intercourse with the farmers themselves. On one point there is a marked difference. If a farmer politely asks a market-hunter not to trespass on his land, he keeps *a civil tongue in his head*, and heeds the warning, because he can not afford to pay $25 in fine and costs for trespass. Not so with your rich man to whom $25 is as a *flea bite*. He often considers himself perfectly justified in abusing the man who is endeavoring to protect his own rights, and indulging in language not *fit for ears polite*.

I was brought up in what is called an *exclusive school*, but I have been here long enough to see that among the many very jolly, good-hearted sportsmen I have met, there will of necessity be, or rather there are, some few of the veriest exclusivists that would do well to mix with the staunchest Conservative or Tory that my country could produce.

Should the challenge be taken up, and the names of the 20 shooters be made known, it is considerable odds that 15 of the 20 will be found, either by direct or collateral evidence, to have joined in a *contest for a money prize*, either with an acknowledged *professional* shot, or with some one who from having engaged in a similar way, with those who may inadvertently have become contaminated, and are, according to the dictum of the *Chicago Field*, to all intents and purposes, professionals themselves.

There can be no half measures; the line, if drawn at all, must be drawn straight, and there is no getting out of it.

If they get tarred with the *professional brush* it will stick to them.

I confess from what I have seen, and as far as I am a judge of shooting, that I do not think any club in the United States, could send ten men that would have any chance with the St. Louis Gun Club.

The question is,

Can the St. Louis Gun Club find ten first class men to come within the conditions? Perhaps they do not intend it to apply to themselves.

Chicago could find the men, perhaps, but their best shots are split up into so many little clubs for the purposes of qualification for team shoots at the State Tournaments, in consequence of the very absurd rule that prevents a club from sending more than one team, that no one club there could furnish ten first class shots.

I would much like to know what some of my blue-blooded countrymen, who shot matches with Bogardus when in England, would say if they were to be called "professional pigeon shots."

I would just casually mention that *gate money* is not known in England, among ordinary pigeon shooters.

The admissions paid by the public go to augment the club funds and provide handsome silver cups and international trophies which are given to be shot for free, weekly, during the whole season.

[From the *Chicago Field*, Oct. 23, 1880.]

"WHAT IS A PROFESSIONAL?—The challenge of the St. Louis Gun Club, published in our last issue, has brought us several inquiries, whom the club consider professional trap shooters. To express the views of the club on that subject is not within our power; but having been also requested to state what we consider constitutes a professional, we have no hesitancy in saying that a man can be regarded as a professional only, who makes his living by trap shooting; in other words, one whose business is trap shooting. The fact that a man has shot for money does not, at the present day, constitute a professional, for if so, there would be very few who shoot at the trap who would not be professionals, as every man who has shot in a tournament would be one. Whether for five dollars or five hundred, does not make any difference. The time was when such a distinction could be made; but, like many other rules, the current of events has completely obliterated it. And how gate money has any bearing on the question, we fail to see. Who, for instance, would claim Mr. W. B. Hauworth and Mr. J. B. Lucas to be professionals? Each has shot for a large stake and for gate money, and is in business and shoots at the trap for pleasure; neither makes his living by it. On this subject we shall have more to say at a future time, as it is a most important one to trap shooters, and is constantly coming up at tournaments and causing much annoyance to those whose only claim to be considered professionals is, that they are a good shot."

It will be seen the bold challenge of the St. Louis Club has opened up a controversy which I hope will be the means, before the trap shooting season commences, of once and for all settling this question. The Club should reply. The above sensible article has just *hit the right nail on the head*, the whole secret lies in the concluding 14 words. Although invitations are issued by advertisements to induce most good and noted shots to attend tournaments in order to draw a crowd of visitors, if a man travels some hundreds of miles, it matters little whether he wears *blue jeans* or the orthodox hunting suit, it is 10 to 1 if he is a good shot, and likely to win a prize or two, that he gets *barred or ruled out*.

Away with such petty, miserable subterfuges, once and forever, and throw the whole thing open to the world in the interest of sport and friendship, as the Louisville Kentucky Sportsmen's Club does. Since the earlier editions the match referred to has taken place. Fifteen men of the Chicago Shooting Club shot against fifteen of the St. Louis Gun Club, at St. Louis, July 7, 1883. The conditions were 30 wild birds each man, viz: 10 at 21, 10 at 26 and 10 at 31 yards rise, plunge traps. St. Louis scored 366 and Chicago 357 out of a possible 450. Certainly not a brilliant score for those distances and one trap. Of the St. Louis team, H. C. Pierce, J. C. Addington and S. C. Edgar, usually fine shots, made poor scores. Abner Price and Abe Kleinman, on the Chicago side, were far below their usual form. I expect to see a different result in the return match whenever it takes place.

I cannot conclude without tendering my heartfelt thanks to a large number of sportsmen and others I have met with during three years hunting in this country, for much kindly expression of good feeling and welcome.

In offering my opinions on little shooting matters, at very likely their full value, 25c., I have no desire to thrust my enthusiasms upon anybody, although I have been accused of doing so, and been told that as an alien I have no right to offer an opinion. No great harm can come from it, however, and some little good might. Not a single word is written with the least unfriendly feeling towards anybody. If I write apparently strongly, it is, perhaps, my failing to *feel what I write, and write what I feel.*

My desire is—

To see class shooting abolished as *encouraging fraud.*

To do away with any distinction between professional and other shooters, as *impracticable and impolitic.*

To discontinue plunge traps, as *puerile* and *unsportsmanlike.*

To adopt ground traps and handicap distances, so as to give every shooter a *fair chance of winning.*

To have birds better cared for and *trapped in good condition*, and the object of this little publication will have been attained.

Go forth my little book, from this thy solitude,
I cast thee on the world—
Where after many days, perhaps, there may spring forth
Such heaps of blossoms that———

"*Bosh*," says a *sporting fiend*, looking over my shoulder while I am writing, "*much more likely to find it lining some new trunk, wrapping up caramels,* or *butter at the corner shop!"*

Away with it to the d——l at once, and let it take its chance! I mean the printers imp of that name, of course. This, after all my trouble? My heart is bursting!! I can no more!!

Very faithfully,

GWYNNE PRICE.

Gwynne Price's New English-Model Improved Ground Trap for Pigeon Shooting.

(See first page of Advertisements.)

PIGEON SHOOT AT SAN FRANCISCO.—"The ground traps of the St. Louis pigeon shooter, author and sportsman, Gwynne Price, were used. They are simple in their mechanism, consisting of wrought-iron boxes, so fixed that as soon as the string is pulled the four sides of the box fall flat. The birds are put in the trap through a round hole in the rear. The traps have a wide grating in front, which allows the bird to see where he is going to, while the narrowness of his temporary prison prevents him from turning round and flying in the face of the shooter. These traps are a vast improvement upon the old-fashioned plunges. In the first place they give the bird some option as to his flight; in the second, they do not give a bird that sudden shock which in a plunge trap makes it hesitate for several seconds and enables a snap shot to shoot at a stationary object; thirdly, shooting birds from ground traps more closely resembles field shooting than any other trap-shooting extant The birds were as a whole a good strong lot, and showed a keen appreciation of the pleasure of living by doing their utmost to escape, even when cut through and through by the merciless pellets. The gold medal of the club was won by that noted field shot, John K. Orr, who, shooting with great coolness and judgment, made a straight score of 12. Next to him came Randall, scoring 10."—[From San Francisco paper, August, 1881.

RULES
FOR
PIGEON SHOOTING
FROM
FIVE GROUND TRAPS,
BY
GWYNNE PRICE,
SPORTSMEN'S CLUB, ST. LOUIS, MO.

———:o:———

The following rules for pigeon shooting from five ground traps, have been very carefully compiled; and it is claimed they will more fnlly meet all requirements, than any before published.

It will be observed that the shooter has been given the benefit of any error or doubt, where interference or wrong doing is suspected.

Thus, if two birds are loosed instead of one, it is calculated to mislead him; so that if he shoots and kills, the bird is scored; but if he misses he will have another bird, because *it may have been done purposely* to annoy or baffle him.

Again, if a bird refuses to fly *in moderate time*, the party supplying it should bear the loss as he is paid for good birds.

It should be clearly understood that it is no part of the duty of a contestant to challenge any bird, or in fact any condition.

It is absolutely the business of the referee to conduct the whole shooting, to notice the holding of the gun, and carry out the general rules, and more than anything, to see that the bird is *fully and fairly on the wing* when shot at, not merely struggling along the ground *using wings and legs,* but to be *legitimately flying*, and if not killed under such circumstances, another bird should be ordered. Also to have every bird gathered before giving his decision. But if a shooter *wilfully* shoots at a sitting bird with his first barrel, it should be scored a lost bird.

All minor matters, such as interference with the shooter or shooting at a bird by a scout, must be left entirely to the referee to decide according to circumstances. His decisions being subject to revision, if unfairly given, as per rule 29.

Apropos of guns and ammunition, the following rule recently adopted by the Hurlingham Gun Club, of London, will not find many admirers in the United States: "After June 17th, the weight of guns shall be limited to 7 pounds 8 ounces, the charge of powder to be limited to 3 1-2 drachms, and soft shot only to be used; no chilled shot or concentrators to be allowed."

RULE 1. *Traps. How Placed.*—Shooting to be from five ground traps, placed five yards apart, the centre trap in a direct line in front of the shooter, and if practicable, the traps so placed that the birds will have the benefit of the wind behind them.

RULE 2. *Traps. How Pulled.*—The number of the trap pulled to be decided by die, or by wads marked 1 to 5, drawn by the referee, after the shooter has advanced to the score, and shown privately to puller.

RULE 3. *Traps. When Pulled.*—When ready, the shooter shall say *pull*, and the trap shall be instantly opened.

RULE 4. *Pulling. Falsely.*—If from any cause more than one bird shall be loosed at the same time, and one or more be killed, one bird shall be scored, and if missed, another bird shall be allowed free of cost.

RULE 5. *Pulling. Notice.*—If the trap is pulled before proper notice from the shooter, he may take or refuse the bird; but *if he shoots*, he must abide by the consequences.

RULE 6. *Holding Gun.*—The gun shall be held fairly down from the shoulder, until the word *pull* is given; and the bird shall be shot at when *fully on the wing*, with the first barrel; after which the second barrel may be used as the shooter likes, without leaving his position.

RULE 7. *Bird. Flying.*—Should the bird refuse to fly *in moderate time*, the referee shall, if requested by the shooter, call a *no bird*, and another shall be trapped without cost, and the die thrown again.

RULE 8. *Bird on Ground.*—A bird deliberately shot at on the ground with the first barrel shall be scored *lost;* but the referee may order another bird, at the shooter's expense, if he has any doubt.

RULE 9. *Size of Gun.*—Guns shall not exceed 11-bore for muzzle-loaders, and 10-bore for breech loaders.

RULE 10. *Shot Charge.*—Charge of shot shall not exceed $1\frac{1}{4}$ oz. Dixon's full measure 1006 or 1007; and no wire cartridges shall be used.

RULE 11. *Shot Challenge.*—Any contestant may challenge the loading of a shooter as he goes to the score, and shall deposit five dollars as a guarantee of good faith. If the charge is found to be unfair, the shooter shall be disqualified; but if his gun was properly loaded, he shall be entitled to the five dollars so deposited.

RULE 12. *Shot Marks.*—A bird shot at when fairly on the wing, and gathered, shall not be challenged for shot marks.

RULE 13. *Miss-Fire.*—A miss-fire will be considered *no shot*, provided the gun is properly loaded and cocked, and another bird shall be trapped at shooter's cost.

RULE 14. *Miss-Fire, First Barrel.*—If the first barrel miss-fire, and the second barrel is used, the bird shall be scored; or if the second barrel miss-fire, another bird shall be had at the shooter's cost; the first barrel being fired *with powder only* after the bird is on the wing.

RULE 15. *Gathering.*—Every bird must be gathered by hand after each shot, either by the shooter or his deputy, in reasonable time, and without going over the boundary line. If a dog is used, the bird shall be scored if once fairly caught, and if the bird should perch within the boundary, the shooter or deputy may assist the dog.

Rule 16. *Boundary.*—If the enclosure is the boundary, and a bird closes his wings on top of the fence, or reaches the roof or cover of any fixed erection inside the grounds higher than the fence, it is a *lost bird.*

Rule 17. *Boundary, Doubtful.*—Should a bird fall within the boundary, and the referee be unable to decide whether it has been over the line, he may order another bird at shooter's expense.

Rule 18. *Fine for Shooting.*—Shooting at a bird within the boundary before it shall have been scored lost, by any other than the shooter, *without his consent*, shall be punishable by a fine of five dollars, and added to the first prize.

Rule 19. *Unloading Guns.*—The gun shall not be fully loaded, or capped, until the shooter is at the mark; and if the second barrel is not used, it must be uncapped or unloaded before returning.

Rule 20. *Danger.*—If a bird flies so that to shoot *in proper time* would endanger life or property, the referee may order another bird without cost.

Rule 21. *Double Birds.*—In shooting at two birds, they may be loosed from one or two traps. Both birds may be killed at one shot, if on the wing. It is not necessary for both birds to be flying at the same time; but if the second bird refuses to fly, two others shall be trapped without cost. The distance should be by handicap, each shooter going in five yards nearer than at single bird shooting.

Rule 22. *Distances.*—Shooting to be all at a given distance, or by a handicap of from 24 to 30 yards rise, according to merit. A winner of any sweepstakes with five or more shooters, shall be put back one yard for each and every win during that day, until he shall have reached the 30 yards limit, and if any shooter at 30 yards wins a like prize, the others shall go in one yard.

Rule 23. *Entry.*—No person shall be allowed to join in a sweepstakes after the first bird in the second round shall have been shot at, unless he arrived on the grounds too late to enter at proper time, and then only by consent of the majority of the contestants.

RULE 24. *Position on Card.*—The position of the shooters shall be decided by drawing, *if demanded*, and each round shot through in regular order; any shooter not being ready in reasonable time, shall forfeit his right in the mateh.

RULE 25. *Sweepstakes.*—Sweepstakes of $1 to be miss and out; $2, 3 birds each, one miss wait; and $5, 6 birds each, two misses wait.

RULE 26. *Winning Penalty.*—A winner of a prize of $100 or more, at one time, shall be put back one yard in his regular handicap for every such win.

RULE 27. *Ties.*—All ties, except in matches, *when all bets are off*, are to be shot off same time, same number of birds, and same distances, unless mutually agreed to be miss and out, or divided; a majority in the ties to rule.

RULE 28. *Division of Stakes.*—Moneys to be divided between the *three best shots*, in the proportion of 50, 30 and 20 per cent., after deducting cost of birds.

RULE 29. *Appeal.*—The decision of the referee shall at all times be upheld, unless on a question of fact *or construction of the rules*, a majority of three-fifths of the shooters shall be in favor of the appellant, by a private ballot, taken by the scorer on the spot, and before another bird is shot at.

These rules are published in a separate form for the pocket. Mailed free for 5 cents, stamps, by GWYNNE PRICE, St. Louis, Mo.

GWYNNE PRICE'S

NEWLY DISCOVERED

LIVER MEDICINE.

The principal ingredient in the composition of this wonderful cure for Chills, Malarial Fever, and *all Liver Complaints*, was found by Gwynne Price when hunting. It is from a plant grown in the bottoms of Illinois and Missouri, which, in combination with several other properties, form together a medicine which acts upon the liver powerfully, yet soothingly, in such a direct and extraordinary manner that *two or three doses only* will accomplish *more than any other remedy* can do in months, and is so harmless that it is just as beneficial and may be taken by a child.

Any ordinary cases of Malarial Fever, Chills, Piles, Costiveness, Biliousness, Dyspepsia, Children's Fevers, etc., cured by two or three doses of the LIFE PILLS, at 35 cents a box.

The most *severe and prolonged* cases of Ague and Chills, and Malarial Fever are cured in 24 hours by the AGUE PILLS, at $1 per box.

QUININE LEMON PILLS, the best tonic, correcting acidity and strengthening the system, to be taken after the other Pills, 50 cents per box.

The dangerous and very prevalent malady, *Costiveness*, the cause of Piles and almost every disease the body is subject to, the surest sign of an inactive and disordered liver and impaired digestion, will be completely and effectually remedied by an occasional dose of the LIFE PILLS. No medicine ever before discovered will so surely cure Costiveness, Diarrhœa, Piles, and all complaints arising from Indigestion and Biliousness.

No Sportsman should be without a supply of these medicines as a part of his outfit on hunting trips, *particularly in Malarial districts*. It is the only remedy ever discovered that will cure Chills and Fever, however severe, in one day.

Instead of reducing the system by a succession of purgative doses, which *weaken and inflame* the bowels, as most so-called liver pills do, this medicine is so *direct and immediate* in its action upon the liver that the appetite is regained in a few hours.

Mailed free for postal order or stamps to

SANGAMON PILLS CO.,

GWYNNE PRICE, MANAGER,

RINKELVILLE, ST. LOUIS, MO.

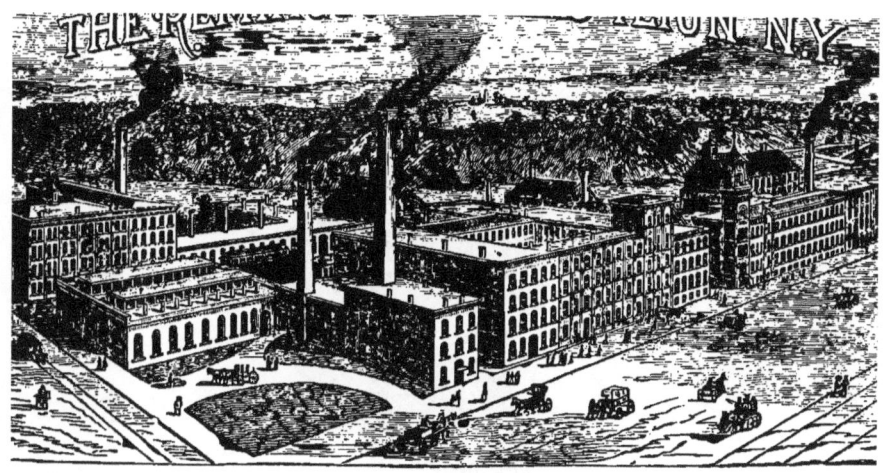

EXTRAORDINARY GLASS BALL SHOOTING,

E.T. Martin Esq of Chicago, defeats Dr. Alexander, breaking 100 Glass Balls out of 101 in 7 minutes & 46 seconds with a REMINGTON $45.00 BREECH LOADER.

Extract from Louisville Courier Journal October 4th 1878.

'Yesterday closed the "Shooting Tournament" that has been going on for several days at Eclipse Park, during which time, Exhibitions of Superior Skill have been shown.

The Contest between Dr. Alexander and E.T. MARTIN was the event of the TOURNAMENT, the latter breaking 100 Balls out of 101 in 7 Minutes and 46 Seconds. Mr. Martin shot a REMINGTON 12 gauge gun, loaded with 4 drachms of Powder and 1 & 1-8 ounces no, 9 chilled shot. He was loudly applauded on his Success.

Louisville Ky. October 6th. 1878

Dear Sir,

Please find score made by me with a REMINGTON $40.00 12 gauge Breech Loader, at shooting match with Dr. Alexander Oct. 4th. 1878. eighteen yards rise, time 7 minutes 46 seconds.

Score—1 1 0 1 1 1 1 1 1 1 1 1 1 1 1 1 1 1 1 1 1 1 1 1 1 1 1 1 1 1 1 1 1 1 1 1 1 1 1 1 1 1 1 1 1 1 1 :
1 1 1 1 1 1 1 1 1 1 1 1 1   1 1 1 1 1 1 1 1 1 1 1 1 1 1 1 1 1 1 1 1 1 1 1 1 1 1 1 1 1 1 1

Very Respectfully

E. T. Martin

Dr. Alexanders score was 100 out of 114. Time 8 minutes 46 seconds.

D. H. LAMBERSON & CO.,

Sole Western Agents for

E. REMINGTON & SONS'

Breech-loading Rifles, Shot Guns, Revolvers, Cartridges, &c.

73 STATE STREET, - - CHICAGO, ILL.
(CENTRAL MUSIC HALL BLOCK.)

FISHING TACKLE, CUTLERY AND SPORTING GOODS OF ALL KINDS.

NEW YORK OFFICE: LAMBERSON, FURMAN & CO., 281 & 283 Broadway.

Send Stamps for Catalogue. This Book mailed on receipt of 25 cents.

www.ingramcontent.com/pod-product-compliance
Lightning Source LLC
Chambersburg PA
CBHW020323090426
42735CB00009B/1379